ADAPTING IN THE DUST

Lessons Learned from Canada's War in Afghanistan

Canada's six-year military mission in Afghanistan's Kandahar province was one of the most intense and challenging moments in Canadian foreign affairs since the Korean War. A complex war fought in an inhospitable environment, the Afghanistan mission tested the mettle not just of Canada's soldiers but also of its politicians, public servants, and policymakers. In *Adapting in the Dust*, Stephen M. Saideman considers how well the Canadian government, media, and public managed the challenge.

Building on interviews with military officers, civilian officials, and politicians, Saideman shows how key actors in Canada's political system, including the prime minister, the political parties, and Parliament, responded to the demands of a costly and controversial mission. Some adapted well; others adapted poorly or – worse yet – in ways that protected careers but harmed the mission itself. *Adapting in the Dust* is a vital evaluation of how well Canada's institutions, parties, and policymakers responded to the need to oversee and sustain a military intervention overseas, and an important guide to what will have to change in order to do better next time.

STEPHEN M. SAIDEMAN is the Paterson Chair in International Affairs at the Norman Paterson School of International Affairs at Carleton University.

UTP insights

UTP Insights is an innovative collection of brief books offering accessible introductions to the ideas that shape our world. Each volume in the series focuses on a contemporary issue, offering a fresh perspective anchored in scholarship. Spanning a broad range of disciplines in the social sciences and humanities, the books in the UTP Insights series contribute to public discourse and debate and provide a valuable resource for instructors and students.

BOOKS IN THE SERIES

ADAPTING IN THE DUST

Lessons Learned from Canada's War in Afghanistan

Stephen M. Saideman

UNIVERSITY OF TORONTO PRESS
Toronto Buffalo London

© University of Toronto Press 2016
Toronto Buffalo London
www.utppublishing.com
Printed in Canada

ISBN 978-1-4426-4695-7 (cloth)
ISBN 978-1-4426-1473-4 (paper)

∞

Printed on acid-free, 100% post-consumer recycled paper with vegetable-based inks.

Library and Archives Canada Cataloguing in Publication

Saideman, Stephen M., author
Adapting in the dust : lessons learned from Canada's war in Afghanistan /
Stephen M. Saideman.

(UTP insights series)
Includes bibliographical references and index.
ISBN 978-1-4426-4695-7 (bound). – ISBN 978-1-4426-1473-4 (paperback)

1. Afghan War, 2001– – Participation, Canadian.   2. Canada – Armed Forces
– Afghanistan.   3. Afghan War, 2001– – Personal narratives, Canadian.
4. Canada – Military policy.   I. Title.   II. Series: UTP insights

DS371.41252.C3S23 2016   958.104'7   C2015-906925-4

University of Toronto Press acknowledges the financial assistance to its
publishing program of the Canada Council for the Arts and the Ontario Arts
Council, an agency of the Government of Ontario.

 Canada Council   Conseil des Arts
for the Arts   du Canada

ONTARIO ARTS COUNCIL
CONSEIL DES ARTS DE L'ONTARIO
an Ontario government agency
un organisme du gouvernement de l'Ontario

Funded by the   Financé par le
Government   gouvernement
of Canada   du Canada

 Canadä

*This book is dedicated to my Ottawa friends, old and new,
who not only greatly informed this project
but made me and mine most welcome in our new home.*

Contents

Figures and Tables

Figures

Tables

Acknowledgments

This book emerged out of a project focused on the North Atlantic Treaty Organization (NATO) and the Afghanistan experience. As I worked with David Auerswald on the larger NATO question, interviewing officials in Australia, New Zealand, and Europe, I was impressed with the way in which others viewed Canada's civilian effort because it contrasted rather strongly with the criticism I was hearing in Canada itself. As a scholar working in Canada, I was frequently asked for my views on the country's Afghanistan effort and started blogging[1] about it to work out my own confusion. Those short posts helped to inspire this book – an effort to understand how Canada carries out its international relations. As it turns out, the question is more complex than I imagined given that the various sectors of the government as well as actors beyond the government performed quite differently during Canada's involvement in Afghanistan. Some adapted better than others to the stresses and challenges of Canada's first counter-insurgency and its first war in quite some time.

One of the biggest contrasts for scholars researching Canada's mission in Afghanistan is the relative accessibility of the Canadian Forces compared to the rest of the government. Readers of this book will notice that many military officers are cited by name, whereas many comments made by civilians are not attributed to specific

---

1 Mostly at saideman.blogspot.ca but also opencanada.org.

individuals but to particular kinds of office holders – senior officials of the Department of Foreign Affairs and International Trade (DFAIT)[2] and the like. The civilians interviewed made it clear that their careers could be harmed if they were directly quoted. The military officers occasionally indicated some caution or asked to make specific comments off the record, but they showed far less concern about the career implications of speaking to a random academic. This raises larger questions, some of which I address in the book, about the communications strategies and accessibility of different government agencies.

To be clear, this variance in openness did affect what I could understand and what I could write. That no one from the Canadian International Development Agency (CIDA) was willing to talk to me on the record and that retired CIDA personnel were willing to talk only off the record means that the agency probably gets short-changed in this book. Fortunately, this approach was not typical as I was able to interview officials in DFAIT, the Department of Public Safety, and other departments. Still, it means that some sources here are not directly attributed. I tried as much as possible to triangulate so that readers could be confident that the anonymous sources were not random cranks but fairly representative. I am grateful to all of those in the Canadian government, as well as those working for other countries, for their time and their perspectives. This book would simply not exist if people had not been patient with the random academic showing up in their offices or meeting them in Ottawa's Byward Market.

My first debt is to David Auerswald, my co-author on the NATO project, who encouraged my deep dives into Canadian defence politics and policy and who was a great sounding board as I tried to figure out this particular case.

This project was made possible by grants from the Social Sciences and Humanities Research Council of Canada, the Canada Research

---

2 As nearly all of this research took place before DFAIT merged with CIDA, I use the older name for Foreign Affairs throughout the book.

Chairs Program, NATO's Public Diplomacy Division, and the late and lamented Security and Defence Forum as well as funds from the Paterson Chair endowment at Carleton University. A series of research assistants – Chris Chhim, Alexia Jablonski, Scott Shaw, Stephanie Soiffer, Ora Szekely, and Lauren Van Den Berg – were of tremendous help throughout the process. Interviews were greatly facilitated by the two arms of the Department of National Defence (DND) – the Security and Defence Forum (now known as the Defence Engagement Program) and the Public Relations branch. I am especially grateful to Anne Therienn, Jamie Gibson, and Aaron Hywarren of the Forum; Susan Christopher and André Berdais of the Montreal Public Relations branch of DND; and Brian McCarthy of Canadian Expeditionary Forces Command. I also greatly appreciate those who helped arrange my participation in a 2007 "opinion leaders" familiarization tour of Kabul and Kandahar: Brenna Morrell, Megan Minnion, and Albert Wong.

I have benefited from discussions with many scholars across Canada, including David Bercuson, Marie-Eve Desrosiers, Jean-Christophe Boucher, David Haglund, Frédéric Mérand, Kim Richard Nossal, Lee Windsor, and Stéfanie von Hlatky. Conversations with Roland Paris were especially illuminating. I am grateful to the contributors to the volume *Elusive Pursuits: Lessons from Canada's Interventions Abroad*, which I worked on concurrently with this book, as they helped to provide a broader perspective on Canada's place in the world.

I received many helpful suggestions and insightful criticisms at presentations over the years at the University of Ottawa, the Conference of Defence Associations Institute, DND, the United States Army War College, Queen's University, Laval University, the Asia-Pacific Civil-Military Relations Centre of Excellence (now renamed the Australian Civil-Military Centre), the Centre for International Governance Innovation, DFAIT, the Atlantic Council of Canada, the University of Waterloo, the University of Calgary's Centre for Military and Strategic Studies, the University of British Columbia, Concordia University, the Centre interuniversitaire de recherche sur les relations internationales du Canada et du Québec, and the University of New Brunswick.

I am extremely grateful to Phil Lagassé, who not only corrected my misunderstandings of how Westminster systems work in our weekend Twitter conversations/arguments but also read multiple versions of the manuscript. His comments were always constructive, pushing me to provide more nuance as well as helping me understand the history and dynamics of Canadian institutions. I owe him many beers for all of his help on this project.

I appreciate the constructive suggestions made by the various reviewers, and I am most thankful for the suggestions and Sherpaship[3] of this book by Daniel Quinlan as well as all of the hard work of the editors and other staffers at University of Toronto Press. I am also very grateful to Stephanie Stone for her careful attention to the manuscript, cleaning up all of my mistakes, and to Kelly McDougall for helping out in that effort, especially tracking down all of the pesky links that seemed to keep moving around.

My greatest debt, of course, is to my wife and daughter, who put up with my travels across Canada and beyond as I conducted the research and then presented my findings. The frequent flyer miles and small gifts from these various trips are small consolation for the time away. For your patience and support, I am and will always be so very grateful.

Of course, all errors that remain in this book are solely my responsibility.

---

3 I was and will always be surprised that DFATD lists *Sherpa* as an official position.

Abbreviations

ANA	Afghan National Army
ANP	Afghan National Police
CBSA	Canada Border Services Agency
CDS	Chief of the Defence Staff
CEFCOM	Canadian Expeditionary Forces Command
CF	Canadian Forces
CIDA	Canadian International Development Agency
CJOC	Canadian Joint Operations Command
COIN	counter-insurgency
CSC	Correctional Service of Canada
CSIS	Canadian Security Intelligence Service
DCDS	Deputy Chief of the Defence Staff
DFAIT	Department of Foreign Affairs and International Trade
DFATD	Department of Foreign Affairs, Trade and Development
DND	Department of National Defence
GDP	gross domestic product
IED	improvised explosive device
ISAF	International Security Assistance Force
JTF2	Joint Task Force 2
KAF	Kandahar Air Field
MP	member of Parliament
NATO	North Atlantic Treaty Organization
NDHQ	National Defence Headquarters

NDP	New Democratic Party
NGO	non-governmental organization
OEF	Operation Enduring Freedom
OMLT	Observer, Mentor and Liaison Team
PRT	Provincial Reconstruction Team
RC-E	Regional Command East
RC-N	Regional Command North
RC-S	Regional Command South
RC-W	Regional Command West
RCMP	Royal Canadian Mounted Police
RoCK	Representative of Canada in Kandahar
SAT-A	Strategic Advisory Team of Afghanistan
SHAPE	Supreme Headquarters Allied Powers Europe
SOF	Special Operations Forces
UN	United Nations
USAID	United States Agency for International Development
WG	Whole of Government

ADAPTING IN THE DUST

Lessons Learned from Canada's War in Afghanistan

chapter one

Introduction

There is no doubt that Canada's mission in Kandahar was the most intense and painful experience in its foreign affairs since the Korean War. While the Canadian Forces (CF) had experienced combat in peacekeeping operations in Croatia, Cyprus, and elsewhere as well as in dropping bombs on Serbia, Afghanistan was the first time that Canada had engaged in sustained, large-scale infantry operations in generations.[1] Not only was the army fully engaged in a difficult campaign on the other side of the world, but much of the Canadian government was also focused on the Afghanistan mission. The Canadian International Development Agency (CIDA) was reoriented from traditional priorities and operations to building schools and markets in Kandahar. The Department of Foreign Affairs and International Trade (DFAIT)[2] was not only meeting with officials in Washington, London, Brussels, The Hague, and elsewhere but also sending officers to the field to help Afghans develop some sort of governance; this is where the first civilian casualty occurred. Other government departments, such as Public Safety, spent considerable resources as well.

The ultimate tally from the mission to Afghanistan exceeded 160 Canadian lives lost, more than 1,000 wounded, and over $20 billion spent.[3] The war will cost much more money over the next 50 years or so as veterans will continue to require disability payments and medical care. As public support declined, those governing with only minority support in Parliament were at some risk. Ministers faced tough questions, and the series of extension votes put the political parties in difficult situations. The media not only had to expend significant resources to cover a distant war but also had to decide how to deal with a variety of sensitive issues, including how to cover the return of the dead. Indeed, the media lost one of its own in Kandahar. In short, the Afghanistan mission created a great deal of pressure back home in Ottawa.

There have been and will continue to be many books published that seek to explain the decisions, the strategies, and the outcomes.[4] There is already a burgeoning literature on the Canadian experiences in Afghanistan, with soldiers writing about their time there.[5] This book's focus is neither on the decisions made in Ottawa or Kandahar nor on what Canadians encountered in Afghanistan. Instead, the premise here is that we can learn a great deal about Canada from what it experienced in Afghanistan and how it reacted. Just as we can learn the qualities of minerals by placing them under pressure, the political forces generated by the challenges of Afghanistan revealed much about how Canadian institutions, parties, and other actors operate. That is, Afghanistan revealed the character of the Canadian political system. The intent in this book is to use the Canadian experience in Afghanistan to understand the politics and processes that shape Canadian politics, foreign policy, and defence strategies – not just in such harsh conditions but also in general, not just in the recent past but also in the years ahead.

During the Canadian involvement in Afghanistan, one often heard officials proclaim in frustration that "Canadians are confused about Afghanistan," as if this should come as a surprise. Of course Canadians were confused about Afghanistan; it is a confusing place, and the outsiders were confused about how best to deal with the conflict. The North Atlantic Treaty Organization (NATO) and other outside actors were confounded by actors who spent as much or more effort criticizing the outsiders as confronting the insurgents, especially Afghanistan's president at the time, Hamid Karzai. The complexity of tribal ties led the United States and others to employ anthropologists to work out the social structures of the country. Moreover, this was not the conventional kind of war, in which one takes more and more territory and destroys more and more of the enemy in order to win. Instead, it was one of counter-insurgency (COIN), and even the experts disagreed about the best ways to measure success. I was at a roundtable a few years ago where a senior NATO officer lamented that they had more than a few dozen metrics (measures) of success but really did not know which ones were the most relevant. How do you know whether more people support the government than the insurgents today compared to yesterday? If they do, what caused such a change?

Thus, Canadians were not alone in being confused about this war in this place. What is more surprising is that they would be confused by how Canada had operated during the war. Some of the questions that arose included:

- Who made the big decisions: the prime minister, the chief of the defence staff (CDS), or Parliament? The extension votes and the debate about the Kandahar decision confused more than they clarified.
- How much of this confusion was due to minority government? Paul Martin and Stephen Harper faced a variety of challenges as they could not rely on a parliamentary majority. Minority government and Canada's first major shooting war in genera-tions occurred simultaneously, so it is hard to figure out how much of the dynamics were due to the challenge of the govern-ing party having to work with a "hung" Parliament.
- What was the role of Parliament? To oversee the military? Or hold ministers accountable? It seemed that the only Afghanistan issue capturing the attention of parliamentarians was the treat-ment of detainees after the CF had transferred them to the local Afghan authorities. While this was an important issue, the near total focus on it raises questions about Parliament's role when the CF is deployed. The struggles regarding this one aspect of the mission also reveal Parliament's limitations.
- What was meant by *Whole of Government* (WG)? Or was it holes in government? The idea that the agencies of government should act in concert was hardly revolutionary, but much rheto-ric was focused on compelling the major agencies involved – the CF, DFAIT, and CIDA – to work together in Kandahar and

back in Ottawa. To say that there was much progress may or may not impress given the rather low starting point.

• What was the role of the CF in defence policy? Much concern was raised about the "militarization" of Canadian foreign policy. General Rick Hillier gained a lot of attention for being (selectively) outspoken, but was civilian control of the military ever in doubt? No, there was no coup in Canada. But one might consider the time as a crisis in Canadian civilian control of the military if the mythology about Kandahar was true – that the military hoodwinked the civilians (the prime minister and Cabinet).

• Was Canada confused because the media did not do its job? Government officials complained that the media covered only the combat and not the redevelopment and governance efforts. Whose fault was that – the media's? Or the government's for restricting officials on the ground to relying on Ottawa-scripted talking points? The media's attention seemed to wax and wane depending on whether the mission was at stake in Ottawa. Did the media reflect or shape the public's views on Afghanistan?

This quick tour demonstrates that there are many questions, and a short book like this can only briefly address them. Again, the focus here is not to explain in detail every dimension of the Afghanistan mission, but to highlight what the events of the past 10 years or so say about the forces and processes that shape Canada's foreign and defence policies of today and tomorrow. It is clear that Canada was not ready for a mission as intense and as complex as Afghanistan. The question now is *whether and how Canada adapted* during the conflict so that it will be better equipped the next time. The answer, alas, is that many of the Canadian political processes and institutions and actors adapted, but often not in positive ways. Key institutions and actors adapted either poorly or not at all. We can find elements of the Canadian scene that adjusted well, that could handle Canada's involvement in a dangerous operation abroad, as this book will document. The pattern tended to be that those who had the greatest number of lives at stake adapted the best. In contrast, those who had only their careers at stake adapted poorly, especially the politicians back in Ottawa.

In the rest of this chapter, I cover some of the basics of the effort and of this book: what it is we are talking about when we think of *the* mission in Afghanistan; and what were the relevant players and institutions shaping Canadian efforts. I then preview the rest of the book.

The Missions

When Canadians speak of *the* mission in Afghanistan, it most likely means the six years in Kandahar from 2005 to 2011, when and where the CF (and some civilians) paid a very high price. This part of the effort was also fairly distinct from the rest of the Afghanistan engagement and from previous Canadian peacekeeping efforts as it involved Canadians waging war – killing people. Thus, this particular part of the Afghanistan mission stands out.

Canada's efforts in Afghanistan went through several distinct stages, as Figure 1.1 below illustrates.[6] Canada first sent Joint Task Force 2 (JTF2), its most secret Special Operations Forces (SOF) unit, in late 2001. This unit caused some controversy by being seen in the process of capturing Afghans and turning them over to the United States. The mis-statements about this led to the end of Art Eggleton's time as defence minister. More publicly, Canada deployed a battalion to Kandahar in early 2002 to assist the Americans as part of the response to 9/11. This deployment was largely uncontroversial as it seemed the least the Canadians could do in the aftermath of the attacks on New York and Washington and as it was a relatively short commitment. The most notable part of that mission was the friendly fire incident on 17 April 2002, in which an American plane dropped bombs on Canadian soldiers, killing four and injuring many others.[7] A less well-known aspect of this deployment was that it operated under very restrictive rules, which largely limited the soldiers to the airfield;[8] any mission "beyond the wire" required a telephone call back to commanders in Ottawa. Lieutenant-Colonel Pat Stogran, commander of the unit in Kandahar, confronted a serious possibility – that he might be restricted from acting even if war crimes were happening in front of him.[9] This mission lasted for six months.

Figure 1.1: From Kabul to Kandahar and Back[10]

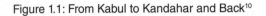

Kabul
Kandahar

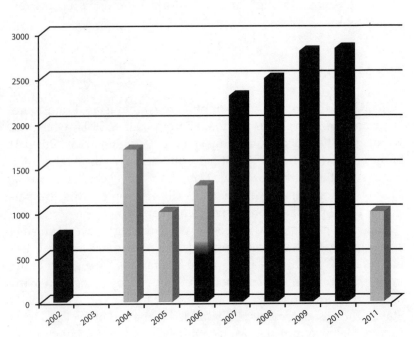

The second deployment occurred in late 2003, to Kabul, and lasted until Canada shifted south to Kandahar in 2005–6. While the first deployment had been part of Operation Enduring Freedom (OEF), an ad hoc US-led operation, the second deployment was part of the International Security Assistance Force (ISAF), which was a multilateral effort, formed under a United Nations (UN) resolution, to help the government of Afghanistan stabilize Kabul. ISAF was not originally a NATO effort, but Canada, as it took its turn to lead the operation, insisted that NATO take it over.[11] Canadian Lt.-General Rick Hillier served as commander of ISAF in 2003–4. While Canadians had taken turns as commanders of a sector of the NATO mission in Bosnia, this was the first time that a

Canadian had served as operational commander of an entire NATO effort.[12]

The third deployment, to Kandahar, lasted from 2005 to 2011, and it is the one that garnered the greatest amount of attention, controversy, and retrospective regret because it was so very challenging and complex. The mission in Kabul had not been that different than the peacekeeping missions of the past: Canadian troops facilitated the disarming of militias and patrolled the largely stable capital. By contrast, Kandahar was a multidimensional effort over a large area with few resources. It put soldiers, officers, and civilian officials into very difficult positions as the mission involved not just combat in a place where the opponents hid among civilians but also governance and reconstruction efforts, which required working with people who had very different interests. While one could take a stand that one would not work with corrupt people, the standards and behaviour were so different that making morally compromising decisions were a daily reality.

Because the Kandahar deployment put the greatest stress on the CF, the government agencies that worked as part of the WG effort, and the politicians back home, it receives more attention in this book (and nearly every other book on the Canadian effort). Still, the key point to keep in mind is that the Canadian effort in Afghanistan started before the battles of 2006 and lasted beyond the end of that part of the conflict, but when Stephen Harper says that this war lasted longer than the two World Wars combined, he is conflating the highly "kinetic" (the military's term for *violent*) Kandahar missions (2002, 2005–11) with the other missions in Afghanistan.

The fourth deployment, between 2011 and 2014, was "Kabul-centric," a carefully tailored training mission to make sure that the CF would not be in harm's way, at least not deliberately. The trainers, unlike those in previous efforts to develop the Afghan army, did not go out on patrol as embedded partners. Instead, all of their activities were at training bases, and the only combat would occur if the training bases were attacked (or if the troops were attacked on the roads between bases). Because there were not enough positions in Kabul, the Canadian trainers were sent to other parts of Afghanistan as well, but *not* Kandahar. This training mission may or may not lead to a more effective Afghan National Army (ANA), but it did succeed in practically eliminating CF casualties and removing Afghanistan from the popular consciousness of Canadians. Indeed, a notable feature of the Canadian training effort was that it did not experience any of the "green-on-blue" attacks in which Afghans being trained attacked their trainers.

In reviewing these four missions, I have omitted a key actor, one that entered Afghanistan before the regular CF units and that may or may not still be there now: the Canadian SOF. Canada keeps its secret units much more secret than the United States does,[13] so it is easy to forget that JTF2 was in Afghanistan in 2001, that it did not face the same constraints on where and how to operate as the regular CF units, and that it may have continued to operate in Afghanistan beyond July 2011. Because these efforts are so secret, they play a much smaller role in Canadian politics, the media, and books like these. There are some implications that will arise in subsequent chapters, but the focus of this book will be elsewhere.

The second significant omission[14] thus far is the purpose of the effort. Four missions took place, but what were their objectives? The first mission, in Kandahar in 2002, was aimed at supporting the United States in its war against Al Qaeda. The subsequent missions had as their formal objective supporting the development of a self-sustaining Afghan government. Questions remain about the real purpose of the Canadian effort – did the government of Canada really care about the stability of Afghanistan? During the course of the missions, leaders and pundits put forth all kinds of justifications, including the plight of women and children, regional stability, the war on terrorism, and others.

The one consistency is that Canada was and is supporting the United States and NATO. Afghanistan plays no role in Canadian foreign policy history and has been relevant to Canada only since September 2001. What is unmistakably consistent is the desire to support international institutions like NATO and maintain a good relationship with the United States. In this, Canada is hardly alone despite the mythology surrounding Kandahar – every member of NATO as well as many other countries showed up in Afghanistan to some degree. Most of them had no intrinsic interest in the country but felt obligated by the NATO treaty or felt compelled by their relationship with the United States. In Chapter 2, comparisons with the rest of the members of ISAF will make clear that Canada had much in common with its allies, a fact that will help to account for why Canadians and others fought and died in Afghanistan.

The Road Ahead

While the focus of this book is on what the Afghanistan mission tells us about Canada, we need to be clear that Canada's experience was not unique. In Chapter 2, I compare Canada to the other countries engaged in Afghanistan, which also had problems with extending their missions, explaining their missions to the public, and trying to build WG efforts under conditions with which most were not familiar – combat. The next step, in Chapter 3, is to address the central question facing Canada now – why Kandahar? – as it tells us much about how Canadian politics operates when engaged in the world. This is an effort to clarify the stakes, interests, and influence of the various actors and institutions in Canada and beyond so that we can assess whether Canada's experience can be used to understand broader dynamics.

Once I have established the context, I will show how minority government shaped how Canada conducted the mission; this will help assess whether Canadian behaviour in combat situations will be the same in all future endeavours or only when Canada has a minority government. Chapter 4 also addresses the role of political parties in Canadian defence and foreign policy and concludes that most, if not all, of the parties performed rather poorly in developing and articulating their stances, leading to a limited impact.

Chapter 5 moves the focus slightly to Parliament as an institution. Across the advanced democracies, legislatures played varying roles in shaping and monitoring the Afghanistan mission. It might be an exaggeration to say that Canada's Parliament had the least influence of any, but it would not be a great exaggeration.

This chapter considers the detainee controversy as it reveals much about both the limited capabilities of parliamentarians and focuses very specifically on a secondary set of issues.

The years in Kandahar had implications for how the central foreign policy and defence institutions operate and cooperate, so Chapter 6 addresses the rhetoric and realities of the WG approach to provide a unified effort. One of the central questions is whether the effort to cooperate, limited as it was, can be sustained in future missions. The answer given in this chapter is that such an effort is unlikely to be repeated.

Given how unbalanced the effort in Afghanistan was, with the military taking a leading role both in Ottawa and in the field, many have raised the spectre of a new militarism in Canada. Chapter 7 addresses the questions of whether the CF violated the proper conduct of civil-military relations during the Afghanistan mission and whether it is likely to do so in the future. To be clear, compared to other democracies operating in Afghanistan, the CF was hardly exceptional in its influence. Moreover, given the overall effect of the Afghanistan experience – much less civilian interest in foreign intervention – there will be fewer opportunities for the military to be in a position to affect foreign policy. Still, the patterns revealed here do resonate elsewhere, such as the tendency to be overly optimistic and to deny problems. These tendencies appeared in Afghanistan and remain to shape discussions about current and future efforts.

Chapter 8 addresses the two key actors outside and constraining government – the media and the public. What did we learn about Canadians from their reactions to the war? Public support declined as casualties mounted, but we need to be cautious about saying that Canadians will oppose any mission that places Canadians at risk as the public might have been just as disillusioned by the other part of the violence dynamic – that Canadian soldiers were killing and not just handing out chocolate bars. The Canadian media did as much to muddle things as anyone else given that its focus tended to swing wildly depending on the debates in Ottawa. While there was some courageous coverage and sacrifices by those embedded with the CF, the editorial decisions back home did not help to provide much clarity. By focusing on the media's attention span during the Afghanistan mission, we can assess how the media will react down the road.

The book concludes by considering the larger lessons to be gleaned from the past dozen years or so. Can Canada engage in combat in the future? Will it engage in combat? What enduring effects did the mission have on Canadian institutions? Did Canada learn and adjust to the difficulties of this effort? Which aspects of the Canadian political process adapted, and which ones adapted well? To preview, the time in Kandahar will have a far greater and wider impact on Canadian foreign and domestic politics than other post–Cold War military interventions.

chapter two

Alone in Kandahar?
Canada in Comparative Perspective

To glean lessons from the experience in Afghanistan, we must first determine how much of the Canadian experience was distinctly Canadian. Canada was not alone in Afghanistan, nor was it even alone in Kandahar. The rest of NATO arrived in Afghanistan, faced many of the same challenges, and responded similarly. Canada, as an advanced democracy, as a member of an alliance, and as a member of the international community, was constrained and compelled by many of the same forces and dynamics that also limited and pushed the United States, the United Kingdom, Denmark, Australia, France, and so on. Canada was not the only country to experience challenges when seeking to extend the mission, nor was it the only country to have to figure out how to handle the transfer of detainees to less than reliable Afghan national security forces. Still, Canada followed its own course to a large degree as NATO set relatively loose parameters within which members could operate.[1] Domestic political dynamics played a crucial role in shaping the mission, as did changes within the CF.

This chapter compares and contrasts key elements of the Canadian experience in Afghanistan with other countries operating there. The focus is placed on the strategies, tactics, and processes on the ground in Afghanistan; on the key NATO dynamics in Brussels and at various headquarters; and finally on the politics in the respective capitals around the world. The aim here is to determine the extent to which the problems Canada faced, and its responses to them, were similar to those of the rest of the countries involved in the effort.

On the Ground

For most of its time in Afghanistan, Canada saw that country through the lens of Kandahar. It was hardly unique in this respect. The Dutch only really saw Uruzgan (an adjacent province); after 2005, the British only had its eyes on Helmand; the Germans only really paid attention to the northern part of Afghanistan; the Italians only cared about the west, etc. Almost every NATO member and partner (non-NATO countries working alongside ISAF, including Australia, New Zealand, Sweden, and others) was focused on its "area of operations," or area of responsibility. Only two actors, aside from the insurgents, paid attention to more than a slice of the country – the governments of the United States, which had troops in every region, and of Afghanistan. As a result, countries evaluated the war and developed their strategies in light of how the war was progressing only in their specific sector. The old parable about blind men each touching a different part of an elephant applies well here. While there were many commonalities among the outside actors, they saw and fought the war differently, depending on both their own domestic political dynamics and the "human terrain" they were dealing with in Afghanistan. Canada's situation was more complex than most given that Kandahar was where the Taliban emerged back in the early 1990s.

The second commonality is that nearly every contingent was far smaller than it should have been, given the demands of the situation (see Table 2.1 below for the sizes of the contingents). Whether countries bought into COIN doctrine or thought they were carrying out peacekeeping, they sent far too few troops to cover the population and terrain. British troops, for example, were constantly calling for more reinforcements despite having a very flexible and forward-leaning Danish battle group in Helmand to assist them. With most of its army committed in Iraq until 2009, the US presence was also inadequate.

When NATO moved out from Kabul to Regional Command South (RC-S) in 2005, political processes combined with military tendencies to foster wishful thinking – that the British, Australians, Dutch, Danes, Americans, Romanians, and Canadians would not face that much opposition. There were conflicting intelligence

Table 2.1 Contingents and Fatalities of Coalition Forces[2]

	Fatalities	Maximum size	Population	Fatalities/ size	Rank, fatalities/ size	Fatalities/ population	Rank, fatalities/ populatie
Albania	1	286	3,002,859	0.35%	25	0.0000%	22
Australia	41	1,660	22,683,600	2.47%	6	0.0002%	9
Belgium	1	607	11,041,266	0.16%	26	0.0000%	26
Bulgaria	0	611	7,327,224	0.00%	27	0.0000%	27
Canada	158	3,079	35,002,447	5.13%	3	0.0005%	6
Croatia	0	320	4,398,150	0.00%	27	0.0000%	27
Czech Republic	10	623	10,505,445	1.61%	13	0.0001%	15
Denmark	43	780	5,580,516	5.51%	2	0.0008%	1
Estonia	9	163	1,339,662	5.52%	1	0.0007%	4
France	86	4,005	65,397,912	2.15%	8	0.0001%	12
Georgia	27	1,561	4,570,934	1.73%	10	0.0006%	5
Germany	54	5,000	81,843,743	1.08%	19	0.0001%	19
Greece	0	170	11,290,067	0.00%	27	0.0000%	27
Hungary	7	582	9,957,731	1.20%	15	0.0001%	18
Iceland	0	11	319,575	0.00%	27	0.0000%	27
Italy	48	4,000	60,820,764	1.20%	16	0.0001%	16
Latvia	3	174	2,041,763	1.72%	11	0.0001%	11
Lithuania	1	260	3,007,758	0.38%	24	0.0000%	23
Luxembourg	0	11	524,853	0.00%	27	0.0000%	27
Netherlands	25	2,200	16,730,348	1.14%	18	0.0001%	10
New Zealand	11	236	4,430,400	4.66%	5	0.0002%	7
Norway	10	580	4,985,870	1.72%	12	0.0002%	8
Poland	40	2,597	38,538,447	1.54%	14	0.0001%	13
Portugal	2	170	10,541,840	1.18%	17	0.0000%	24
Romania	21	1,949	21,355,849	1.08%	20	0.0001%	14
Slovakia	3	309	5,404,322	0.97%	22	0.0001%	20
Slovenia	0	80	2,055,496	0.00%	27	0.0000%	27
Spain	34	1,606	46,196,276	2.12%	9	0.0001%	17
Sweden	5	500	9,482,855	1.00%	21	0.0001%	21
Turkey	14	1,840	74,724,269	0.76%	23	0.0000%	25
United Kingdom	453	9,500	62,989,550	4.77%	4	0.0007%	3
United States	2,349	100,000	313,914,040	2.35%	7	0.0007%	2

reports,[3] and countries tended to discount the more pessimistic ones. Indeed, the ups and downs of the extended Dutch decision-making process to agree to deploy troops swung in part due to these reports. Each of the countries that sent troops to southern Afghanistan started with smaller contingents, which they reinforced over the years. The British, for example, started with fewer than 5,000 and peaked at over 9,000. The Dutch started out with around 1,000 and almost doubled that. The Canadians moved from under 2,000 to nearly 3,000. This was a common approach among NATO allies: initially committing too few and adding as few as possible over time.

Why was this the case? Wishful thinking played a role. Costs also played a role. The logistical demands of feeding, watering, arming, and supplying troops in a distant, landlocked country devoid of most infrastructure were intense. The United States estimates that it cost nearly $1 million per soldier per year when he or she was deployed to Afghanistan (or Iraq).[4] While the costs per soldier varied among the advanced democracies, this equation provided a clear budgetary incentive to keep the size of the force as small as possible, even before the fiscal crises after 2008. Many argued that NATO needed a limited "footprint" in Afghanistan given the xenophobia that existed among the Afghans. Most important, there were political imperatives to keep the forces small. Votes in many parliaments produced "force caps," which limited the number of soldiers that could be in Afghanistan at any given time. While this did not apply to Canada or countries with majorities in parliament, coalition governments generally imposed specific limitations on their deployments, including the number of troops involved in a mission.[5]

The third feature common among the countries participating in ISAF was that they were ill equipped for the operation. While Canada received much criticism for arriving in Kandahar without transport helicopters, most of the contingents lacked "tactical" heavy lift. That is, most countries brought too few helicopters to Afghanistan, and this meant increased reliance on roads that were in poor shape even before they were seeded with improvised explosive devices (IEDs). Germany, responsible for leading the entire northern region of Afghanistan (Regional Command North, or RC-N), had only six helicopters for transportation.[6] Italy had a similar number for Regional Command West (RC-W). The short-fall of helicopters in Afghanistan became a major obsession for military and civilian leaders in NATO, leading to some innovation to create a multinational pool of helicopters. Only the United States and perhaps the British showed up in Afghanistan with enough "lift."

Again, why did this happen? Some countries simply had not invested adequately in helicopters, while some had invested in helicopters that could not operate in the dust or negotiate the to-pography of Afghanistan. Others may have sent only a few heli-copters as a way to manage risk – fewer helicopters meant limited range, less aggressive patrolling, and fewer operations. One rea-son Canadian leaders chose Kandahar was that it was a major hub, with plenty of helicopters. Ultimately, the British and the Americans gave the Canadians a lift when their helicopters were not engaged elsewhere and/or if the Canadian mission was a priority, and they provided medical evacuation when the CF incurred casualties. Still, the shortage of helicopters in Afghanistan generated some friction among the contingents.

Canada was also similar to many other nations in terms of what it did on the ground. The three primary formations of the CF were the Provincial Reconstruction Team (PRT); the Observer, Mentor and Liaison Team (OMLT, pronounced "omelette");[7] and the battle group. Many NATO countries ran or co-led PRTs, with only a few opting out – notably France. The PRTs were an innovative strategy to tie together the various efforts – improving security, governance, and development – in spots all over Afghanistan. NATO had very little control over any of the PRTs, and the Afghan government complained about how little coordination there was between the PRTs and the local governments.[8] Each country ran its PRT accord-ing to national plans developed in its own capital. Only late in the war did NATO try to build some coherence among the PRTs, but this risked upsetting the WG efforts in the various national capitals as some parts of government found some NATO priorities more compelling than others (see Chapter 6).

It was strange to hear generals asking for more "omelettes" in Afghanistan, but they were a key part of the training effort. Many countries embedded relatively small numbers of troops into *kandaks* – Afghan infantry units of 600 to 800 soldiers. These embedded troops proved to be important as they provided critical linkages, through their liaison function, to air and artillery support, medical evacuation, logistics, and more. Through mentoring, they provided leadership to Afghan troops. While most NATO countries participated in this effort (the Danes were reluctant and late), they varied significantly in the flexibility of their OMLTs. More than a few refused to let their team of embedded mentors accompany their assigned *kandak* when they moved out of a specific area. This was a problem because the Afghan units were controlled by the Afghan government and could deploy anywhere in the country. German mentors stayed behind if their *kandak* left RC-N, and Germany was not unique in this restriction. Some countries could deploy their OMLT outside their area of responsibility if they received permission.

France was late in sending its OMLT to Kandahar after the first Sarposa prison break because a telephone call had to be routed home and up to the top of the chain of command – to President Sarkozy – before its OMLT could move.[9] This delay was significant as the Canadian commander, Brigadier-General Denis Thompson, had to replace the missing mentors with American marines. Lacking an established relationship with these new mentors, the *kandak*, once it encountered Taliban resistance, fell apart and fled. The next day, with the recently arrived French in place, the *kandak* successfully participated in the operation.[10]

Canada was a bit different than most countries as its OMLTs could and did accompany its *kandak*s out of Kandahar. Even before this, Canada proved itself willing to move elements of the battle group to Helmand and Uruzgan as needed, especially in the early days of the Kandahar mission.

Speaking of the battle group, there was much variation in the size of a country's contingent (see Table 2.1 above); this meant that many, but not all, participants had enough troops to send significant forces out beyond the wire to engage the adversary. However, many of these contingents had restrictions limiting their ability to carry out offensive operations. The Canadian battle group faced the same challenges and risks as other contingents: seeking to disrupt the insurgents, clearing territory for whatever follow-on force Afghanistan would provide, and patrolling throughout its areas of responsibility. Because Canada was in one of the toughest locations (Helmand had a higher pace of violence for much of the war, and parts of eastern Afghanistan were notoriously difficult), Canada paid a very high price in blood. Yet other countries also faced significant casualties, with the Americans, British, and Danes suffering relatively high casualties compared to the rest of NATO (see Table 2.1).

Finally, each country faced the same difficult problem: how to deal with detainees?[11] This was not a new problem as Canada and its partners had occasionally had to detain people in Bosnia and Kosovo. In the former, one could turn prisoners over to the Bosnian government or to the United States, while in the latter, the United States had had a very large prison that could hold those detained by NATO countries. In Afghanistan, however, using the US prison was no longer feasible as a result of the Abu Ghraib scandal, stories of torture at Guantanamo Bay, reports of rendition, and other events, which had eliminated the United States as a legitimate option. Yet NATO countries were not accustomed to building their own prisons, only temporary detainment facilities.[12] In addition, despite Afghanistan having limited capacity in many ways, it was, and is, a sovereign country and would ultimately take possession of those Afghans picked up by NATO forces.

Unfortunately, Afghanistan did not have the same kind of norms for treatment of prisoners as Canada and the other Western countries participating in ISAF. Thus, there was a real risk that those Afghans arrested by Canadian, Danish, or German troops might be beaten after they were turned over to the Afghan authorities. Convincing the Afghans to commit to treating prisoners appropriately was an enduring problem, and not just for the Canadian contingent. As a result, countries tended to sign bilateral agreements with Afghanistan with varying levels of guarantees and oversight processes. Yet the problem was never solved, with reports of prisoner abuse continuing long after the Canadians left Kandahar.

In sum, Canada's combat experience in Afghanistan was not at all unique. Canada did occupy some pivotal terrain and played a significant role, but it was hardly the only country engaged in combat against a difficult foe. Other countries led in other difficult spots, such as the British in Helmand and the Americans in eastern Afghanistan. Nearly all countries showed up with insufficient troops and insufficient equipment and were perhaps overly optimistic about the prospects of the mission. None were prepared to deal with detainees after the credibility of US facilities had been undermined.

In the Alliance

Perhaps Canada's sense of isolation in Kandahar was due to a poor understanding of how NATO operates. Despite being the most institutionalized, enduring, and capable alliance, the organization does not actually obligate any member to do anything. The famous Article V, which says that an attack upon one member will be viewed as an attack upon all, includes an opt-out clause that allows each country to respond to the attack as it "deems necessary." In the initial response to 9/11, the first time Article V was ever invoked, NATO sent planes to fly over American cities during major events (the World Series, the Super Bowl, New Year's Eve, etc.) to help patrol, but several nations chose not to participate in this least risky effort. Yes, every NATO member did show up in Afghanistan, but many sent only token contingents. For instance, despite spending a higher percentage of its gross domestic product (GDP) on defence than most NATO members, and despite having one of the largest armies, Greece, for much of its time in Afghanistan, deployed fewer than 20 soldiers; at its maximum, its force never exceeded 0.2 per cent of its army (see Table 2.2 below).

NATO operates by developing a list of units and assets that are needed for an operation, and then the officers at Supreme Headquarters Allied Powers Europe (SHAPE) ask for donations. One officer at SHAPE put it this way: "Force generation is begging."[13] The list is never entirely filled.[14] When countries do agree to contribute units to a NATO mission, they do not turn over complete

Table 2.2 The Size of the Commitment[15]

	Maximum size of contingent	Size of army, 2012	Contingent/army	Rank
United States	100,000	641,470	15.59%	1
Latvia	174	1,137	15.30%	2
Netherlands	2,200	20,836	10.56%	3
United Kingdom	9,500	99,950	9.50%	4
Canada	3,079	34,800	8.85%	5
Georgia	1,561	17,767	8.79%	6
Denmark	780	9,925	7.86%	7
Sweden	500	6,718	7.44%	8
Norway	580	8,900	6.52%	9
Australia	1,660	28,246	5.88%	10
Hungary	582	9,911	5.87%	11
Poland	2,597	46,900	5.54%	12
Slovakia	309	6,230	4.96%	13
Czech Republic	623	12,833	4.85%	14
Belgium	607	12,544	4.84%	15
New Zealand	236	4,905	4.81%	16
Germany	5,000	105,291	4.75%	17
Romania	1,949	41,500	4.70%	18
Bulgaria	611	16,304	3.75%	19
Italy	4,000	107,500	3.72%	20
Albania	286	8,150	3.51%	21
Lithuania	260	8,200	3.17%	22
Estonia	163	5,300	3.08%	23
France	4,005	130,600	3.07%	24
Croatia	320	11,390	2.81%	25
Spain	1,606	78,121	2.06%	26
Luxembourg	11	900	1.22%	27
Slovenia	80	7,600	1.05%	28
Turkey	1,840	258,700	0.71%	29
Portugal	170	25,701	0.66%	30
Greece	170	87,441	0.19%	31
Iceland	11	0	0.00%	32

control. Each country has a variety of means to influence how their troops are used in the field or in the skies, including selecting compliant commanders, tailoring the mission and the force to limit how they can be used, engaging in intrusive oversight, and providing incentives for the commanders to ensure compliance with the national chain of command.[16] The tool that received the greatest media attention was the caveat. Countries would impose restrictions on how their forces could be used, sometimes telling NATO and sometimes not. Thus, many contingents could not operate outside their area of responsibility, some could not operate at night, others were not supposed to work with certain allies, and so on. Caveats like these garnered much attention at NATO summits.

For NATO to function, contributions must be voluntary, and national control must be maintained. Because the organization operates by consensus, countries must not be forced to give up control of their troops; otherwise, some (or all) would never agree to a mission in the first place. Allowing opt-outs at every stage is necessary to gain the consensus needed to authorize a mission. Countries can then participate as much as they choose and even change their minds along the way, increasing or decreasing their commitment and their flexibility. NATO's rules of engagement are written rather broadly so that countries can choose how much they want to do.

So what incentives are there to participate more rather than less? First, countries vary in how much they care about any particular mission. The United States, for example, was willing in 2009 to ramp up its efforts in Afghanistan because it wanted to achieve success, and President Obama had signalled during the election campaign that the Afghan mission would be a priority.

Second, countries will sometimes seek to have larger, more engaged contingents sent to a NATO operation in order to influence the course of it. Sending a smaller force means that one can be only a "strategy consumer," compelled to follow the lead of the other countries. It used to be the case that decision-making for NATO operations was purely a matter of size. For example, the five largest contributors to the Balkans missions (the United States, France, the United Kingdom, Italy, and Germany) would meet to plan the next steps in the effort. But in Afghanistan, it was a matter of not just size but also where and how the forces were committed. Germany sent more troops than nearly any other country (except the United States and the United Kingdom), but because it was committed in a relatively less violent area and its troops faced a variety of restrictions that reduced their impact, the Germans did not have as much influence on the course of the overall mission. Canada was among the more significant contributors and, thus, gained more influence over the effort, as Paul Martin and General Rick Hillier intended (see Chapter 3).

Third, countries may be less interested in the effort itself and more in investing in a relationship. One of the striking facts is that some of the more significant contributors to the ISAF effort were not members of NATO: Australia, Georgia, New Zealand, and Sweden; instead, as Table 2.2 indicates, three of the top 10 contributors were "partners." The logical explanation is that these countries sought to help the United States so that the Americans would be indebted to them. This was clearly the case for Australia as nearly every interview I conducted in Canberra and Sydney in 2010 indicated that Australians did not see Afghanistan as a major concern. Instead, they were deeply interested in investing in their relationship with the United States as China was becoming a bigger challenge in the Pacific. The same was largely true for New Zealand. Georgia, given its desire to join the alliance, was looking not only for American support but also to earn its NATO credentials.

NATO members generally felt an obligation to send troops as the Afghan mission was connected to the attack on the United States on 9/11 and to Article V of the Washington Treaty (NATO's founding document). To refuse to participate was simply not a viable option.

In this, therefore, Canada was not alone. The key locus of decision-making for every country was its own national capital and not NATO headquarters in Brussels or Mons, Belgium, where the military headquarters of NATO is based. For much of the war, there was little capacity or support for coordinating efforts beyond the provincial level. RC-S, which included Kandahar, had very little ability to run operations until the British sent General Nick Carter, along with a division headquarters (a much larger staff plus infrastructure), in late 2009. This coincided with General Stanley McChrystal's efforts to provide greater unity of effort, with the aim of creating regional operations and limiting the development of provincial fiefdoms. This met with considerable resistance as countries varied quite widely on how much they were willing to go along with NATO's plans. To understand how each country behaved in Afghanistan, we need to look at what was happening domestically in each.

At Every Home

While each country's leadership faced different incentives and constraints, there were common dynamics and challenges in many national capitals. The war was not easy for any political actor, whether it was a president, a prime minister, a coalition partner, or an opposition party. There was a constant stream of decisions to make, events to understand and explain, and sacrifices in blood and treasure to justify or criticize. Canadian politicians were not the only ones under great pressure; all democratic elites were accountable for the mixed fortunes of their contingents in harm's way and for the budgetary impact of the effort. With the war lasting longer than expected, being more kinetic than planned, and becoming more costly in terms of lives and dollars than advertised, the public and media outlets across Europe and North America began asking tough questions.

Many politicians faced a particularly difficult challenge – how to govern without sufficient support. Canada was not the only minority government at war in Afghanistan. Denmark had two centre-right coalition partners fall short of having a majority, so these two parties had to rely on a third party to pass legislation. The same was true for the Dutch, the Australians, and the New Zealanders. It is striking that, in many of these democracies, the inability of the opposition parties to get along actually empowered the leaders of minority governments. These prime ministers, Stephen Harper among them, could play the various opposition parties off against each other, at least for a while.

The Netherlands was a key exception as its minority coalition parties could not drum up reliable support from opposition parties; this transformed the initial decision to deploy, and all subsequent decisions, into extended dramas. Until the last minute, the outcome of each vote was uncertain; the dithering took just about all year in 2005–6 to result in sending troops to Uruzgan. In 2010, the Dutch government fell over a vote to extend the mission beyond 2010,[17] thereby becoming the first major ISAF contributor to withdraw from its area of responsibility.

Much of the party politics in these countries reflected public opinion. Canada was not the only country with an ambivalent population; indeed, it was solidly in the middle in terms of public support for much of the effort.[18] As in the other democracies, public opinion soared in favour of the mission in its earliest stages, but as time wore on and casualties mounted, support waned considerably. This dynamic, common to many democracies throughout history,[19] was generally seen across the alliance.

Distinctly Canadian?

It should be clear that much of what occurred in Afghanistan and the impact at home were experiences shared by many, if not most, of the allied countries. The first thing to realize, then, is that much of what we can learn from Canada's experience is not just about how Canada handles modern warfare but how developed democracies address such challenges. While the premise of this book is to ascertain Canada's character from how it reacted under the pressure of Afghanistan, some of these attributes and tendencies are not solely Canadian. Still, countries did not anticipate or react identically, and they managed their participation in the war in varying ways. The key differences between Canada and its partners will set the agenda for the rest of this book.

Canada is distinct in that its decision to deploy troops became controversial mainly in retrospect. Whereas the Dutch hotly debated the decision to go to southern Afghanistan before they sent troops, the Canadian public debate began in earnest only after the price of that decision began to become apparent. There is still much confusion over who drove that decision and who has authority to make such decisions, as we shall see in the next chapter.

Canada was not the only minority government with troops under fire in Afghanistan, but it was the only one that adopted a Manley Panel–type process, whereby the government gave an independent panel much sway in shaping the rest of the mission. In 2007, Stephen Harper asked a senior Liberal, John Manley, to assemble a panel to assess the mission and whether it should be extended past 2008. The Manley Panel and its findings influenced not only the extension vote in 2008 but also the implementation of the WG effort (see Chapter 6). We can read much into the Independent Panel on Canada's Future Role in Afghanistan[20] – that it was an effort by Harper to divide the Liberals, that it was a scheme to impose civilian control over the military, that it gave the Liberals influence over the mission, that it gave the military a tool to procure the systems it needed to fight the war, and so on.

While Canada shares institutional features with its Westminster cousins (the United Kingdom, Australia, New Zealand), with defence committees operating in the dark (without security clearances),[21] it was nearly alone in fixating on a single issue (treatment of detainees); this situation revealed how little members of Parliament (MPs) understood the mission and how little ability they had to hold the government accountable (see chapters 4 and 5). To be fair, this fixation may have also been due to how handy the detainee issue was for the opposition as it sought to score points against the government.

Frustration with WG efforts was widely shared across the alliance. Indeed, many countries looked to Canada as being relatively successful in providing a unified effort in Kandahar. But achieving this level of success was not easy, nor was it inevitable, and the effort back home to have the government agencies work together was both difficult and short-lived.

One of the most surprising aspects in which Canada differed from many of its allies was how much of the decision-making seemed to come from within the military. Not only that, but the CF seized on this situation as an opportunity to dispel the peacekeeping myth that had shaped Canadian attitudes towards it.[22] Does this mean that Canada now suffers from a bout of militarism? Is there a crisis in Canadian civil-military relations, with the CF becoming too powerful?

The answer largely depends on where the public stands. While the public in all of NATO's member countries were confused by the war, Canadians faced an identity crisis of sorts, given the power of the peacekeeping identity. To preview the penultimate chapter of this book, the Canadian public was and is underrated. While many Canadian actors and institutions were not ready for the war and showed limited adaptation throughout the conflict, the Canadian public caught up to events quickly, overcame its identity crisis, and adapted to the confusing events and reporting from both Afghanistan and Ottawa.

chapter three

Considering the Kandahar Conundrum

It should come as no surprise that much retrospection and revision have been dedicated to Canada's decision to deploy to Kandahar. Canada paid a far higher price in blood in that one province than in the rest of Afghanistan and more than it had incurred in decades of military interventions around the world. The decision to go to Kandahar shaped the course of Canadian foreign and domestic politics for the next several years, and the mythology around that decision will influence how Canadians think about the entire mission well into the future.

There are a couple of common explanations as to how Canada found itself deployed in Kandahar: Canada moved too slowly and was stuck with the least attractive portion of Afghanistan; or the military hoodwinked Prime Minister Paul Martin. The reality is that the mission to Kandahar matched rather well the aspirations of not just the CF but also DFAIT and, more important, those of the prime minister. Each actor sought to redefine its own role as well as Canada's role in the world, and each saw Kandahar as an opportunity to accomplish those ambitions. Despite the challenges and failures, Martin, General Rick Hillier, and the others were not wrong – Kandahar altered the way in which Canadians viewed various institutions, and the mission did change how the world viewed Canada. Whether it was worth the cost is a question I address in this book's conclusion, but we may not really know for a decade or two.

In this chapter, I address the various contending explanations for the deployment decision. To be sure, each has some merits, but the keys here are that the decision did not deviate from what one would consider to be Canada's national interests and that other countries made very similar decisions.[1] Once again, we need to keep in mind what other countries were doing as every other member of NATO was participating in this effort; staying out of the conflict entirely was simply not an option. The question was not if, but where, the Canadians would deploy and in what capacity.

The Emerging Conventional Wisdom: Slow and Manipulated

Initially, NATO was restricted to Kabul and the surrounding region. When it moved to take responsibility over the rest of Afghanistan, it did so progressively, going first into the easier, less dangerous regions of RC-N, going second into the similarly less kinetic RC-W. This counter-clockwise expansion continued, with Canada, the United Kingdom, and the Netherlands moving into RC-S and rotating the leadership of the NATO effort there. The last part of Afghanistan, Regional Command East (RC-E), which was about as violent as RC-S, remained in mostly American hands, although it then moved under the NATO chain of command.

This pattern suggests that the countries that moved quickest in this game of musical chairs received the better (easier) assignments. It is natural, then, to suggest that Canada was assigned to Kandahar because it was slow to act. John Manley, suggesting that Paul Martin was indecisive, finds this explanation to be persuasive.[2] Indeed, given the rotation patterns set up at the time, it seemed somewhere between unlikely and impossible that Canada could participate in the first or second stages of NATO's expansion to the rest of the country.[3] However, Kandahar was not the only slice of the country left to claim. Canada could have ended up in RC-W under Italian leadership in Herat or Chaghcharan, even if it meant arriving somewhat after Italy's deployment. Indeed, much of the discussion in 2005 was between Kandahar and Herat. It is also possible that Canada could have received an assignment in RC-E – not all of the selections there would have been as dangerous as Kandahar.

The prevailing argument in Canada is that the military, driven to placate the United States, manipulated Prime Minister Paul Martin into committing to Kandahar. This argument is best articulated by Canada's most prominent scholar of international relations, Janice Gross Stein, and by a former adviser to Liberal defence ministers, Eugene Lang.[4] They focused on "Hillier's extraordinary powers of persuasion."[5] With the Canadian military looking south for approval and a DFAIT concerned about too many negative responses to American requests (ballistic missile defence, Iraq), Hillier, argue Stein and Lang, convinced a very reluctant Paul Martin, whose priorities were elsewhere, to commit to the Kandahar deployment.

> The burden of my message to General Hillier was that our commitment in Afghanistan had to be shaped in the context not only of other current commitments but potential new ones. He assured me that he understood, and that whatever the next tag might be in our Afghanistan mission, it would not preclude our capacity to deploy elsewhere.[6]

This account suggests that Hillier underplayed the risks and that Martin was essentially bullied into the decision by Hillier's enthusiasm. Indeed, Martin began to oppose the mission once his party lost to the Conservatives in 2006, and the justification for this opposition seems to give more credence to the notion that he was hoodwinked. He and other Liberals gave three reasons for their new-found opposition to the mission, which they had initiated.

- Hillier had either lied or underestimated the extent of the mission so that it precluded possible Canadian participation in efforts in Darfur or Haiti or to keep a Middle East peace between Israel and Palestine.
- The mission involved far less development and reconstruction than promised.
- The Liberals had expected Canada to commit to only a year and that other countries would eventually rotate into Kandahar.[7]

Regarding the first reason, yes, the mission expanded and re-quired more resources than expected. But, as it turns out, Canada was able to participate in Afghanistan and still respond to emer-gencies in Haiti. While Martin cares a great deal about Africa, it seems strange to focus so much on a mission to Darfur that was not in the cards.[8] But if it had been, NATO was occupied, so Canada would have been going to Darfur without its allies, thus placing itself in a very vulnerable position – if Sudan ever allowed a seri-ous peace operation there.[9] The strangest aspect of the reference to a Mideast peace is that there has been no such peace agreement, and it is obviously *not* the case that the key obstacle was the lack of Canadian peacekeepers.

The second reason invites the criticism that it ignores the reality that the "enemy got a vote" in how much governance and devel-opment were being carried out. Specifically, Glyn Berry, a senior DFAIT official, was killed in January 2006, leading the government to place tight restrictions on what non-military personnel in Kandahar could do. I return to this in subsequent chapters, but the point here is that Martin probably would have done the same thing: as violence spiked in Kandahar, he would have limited what DFAIT and CIDA could do.

The third reason raises the following justification for opposition: "I learned a valuable lesson: whatever commitment we made, we needed to have an end date and an assured rotation out."[10] Instead, Martin's successor, Stephen Harper, committed Canada beyond a year so that it could not rotate in and out. The notion that Canada could hop in and out of Kandahar – which seems to have been a common misconception at the time – was naive for several rea-sons. First, it was clear that there were no other countries ready to fill in for Canada after its first year was over. Second, no other country seemed to be expecting a rotation scheme. The only rota-tion was in who commanded a sector. In Bosnia, Canada had ro-tated in and out of command in the sector it shared with the British and Dutch, but Canadian forces had remained on the ground throughout the mission. The plan for RC-S in Afghanistan was the same – the British, the Dutch, and the Canadians would rotate command of RC-S, but each country would keep troops in their respective areas of responsibility for the foreseeable future. Third, in a conflict like this, in which countries were given primary responsibility over an area and engaged with the local populace to foster development and governance, an ever-changing roster of nations would inevitably undermine those efforts. It was hard enough to develop consistency in the effort as individual units from one country rotated in and out. It would have been incredibly counterproductive to have countries do the same, disrupting the relationships needed to pursue the mission. Thus, there is a logical contradiction between the desire for rotations and the desire for more reconstruction and governance work.

Clearly, Martin would have preferred to focus military resources and his attention elsewhere. He cared then and to this day far more about Africa.[11] He was almost certainly reluctant to continue a Jean Chrétien initiative, preferring instead to start his own. There is something to the idea that Martin might not have chosen Kandahar were it not for other factors in play. It is also probably the case that the stances taken after losing the election were aimed at enabling the Liberal Party to oppose and/or criticize the government. As we shall see in the next section, those factors were not simply the wishes and whims of Rick Hillier but also part and parcel of Canada's national interests.

Kandahar and Canada's National Interests

The reality is that Rick Hillier was not alone in advocating for Kandahar. Substantial elements within DFAIT considered that Canada would derive greater value from deploying to Kandahar than elsewhere in Afghanistan,[12] a stance that is harder to substantiate these days as that agency has sought to avoid blame for this decision.[13] Still, DFAIT concurred with the basic outlook that the mission would elevate Canada's standing much more than moving to a "strategic backwater" like Chaghcharan.[14] Indeed, in conversations with several individuals who worked in and near DFAIT at the time, it is clear that Christopher Alexander, who served as Canada's ambassador to Afghanistan and then as the

UN deputy special representative, was seen as an important advocate of deploying to Kandahar. On the decision to deploy the PRT to Kandahar, which shaped the decision about the battle group, Stein and Lang include this quote from Alexander: "We [the Canadian embassy] recommended Kandahar from the start.... Everyone knew it was going to be a pivotal province."[15] Alexander was in good company in DFAIT as other key actors in the agency also viewed Kandahar as a more visible locale where Canada could make a difference and raise its profile in the world.[16]

To understand the decision to deploy to Kandahar, it is necessary to keep in mind what has already been established here: like every other member of NATO, Canada was going to be committed somewhere in Afghanistan. The mission was squarely in its national interests by supporting the United States, participating in NATO, and making a difference in the world.[17] The question was not if, but rather when and where and how.

Placating the United States Is a Bad Thing?

The common view of the Kandahar decision makes it appear as if doing something that will please the United States is somehow distinct from, or even contradictory to, Canada's national interests. Stein and Lang argue that "a new consensus, led by DND [Department of National Defence], was rapidly emerging in Ottawa: Canada, and in particular the Canadian Forces, needed to do something significant for Washington – something that the Pentagon really valued – to compensate for the refusal to participate in Ballistic Missile defence."[18] This discussion makes it seem as though improving relations with the United States is somehow not in Canada's interest, that Canada should be expected to not sacrifice other interests for the sake of maintaining good relations with the United States. However, Canada does have a strong interest in buttressing its relationship with the United States given its geographic location, economic interdependence, and limited defence budgets.

Again, Canada is not alone in this. Other countries invested a great deal in the Afghanistan effort because it was important to the

United States, and, in turn, maintaining a strong relationship with the United States was important to those countries. Australia sent a significant number of troops to Afghanistan even though it does not belong to NATO. In interviews I had in Canberra and Sydney in March of 2010 with senior military officers and civilian officials, it was clear, and unabashedly so, that Australia had no intrinsic interests in Afghanistan but saw its participation as investing in good relations with the United States. The New Zealanders, Danes, Dutch, and others reported the same interest in the Afghanistan mission – it was important to the United States, and one had to support this ally in this priority.[19]

In It Together

But this was not just about the United States; it was also about the Atlantic Alliance: it cannot be emphasized enough that every NATO country sent troops to Afghanistan. "In short, alliance dynamics matter. They do not determine outcomes per se, but they heavily condition them."[20] The Kandahar decision came just four years after the 9/11 attacks, when Article V of the NATO treaty – an attack upon one is considered an attack upon all – had been invoked for the first time. The pattern of complete NATO attendance in Afghanistan (even if the burden was unevenly shared)[21] coincided with a second pattern – that of Canadian participation in previous NATO efforts.[22] During the Cold War, Canada had dedicated a significant part of its military planning, spending, and training to the defence of Europe and the North Atlantic. Canada had spent much time, effort, and money in Bosnia, in the skies over Kosovo and Serbia, in the Libyan mission in 2011, and in the NATO mission to thwart piracy off the shores of Somalia. Canada has been a significant contributor to every significant NATO mission in the alliance's history, so opting out of Afghanistan in 2005 was close to unimaginable. Indeed, even as Canada was leaving Kandahar in 2011, Stephen Harper apparently felt sufficient pressure to support the alliance that he started a new, less risky training mission in Afghanistan.

Why is NATO such a consistent thread in Canadian foreign and defence policy?[23] There are two main reasons for its importance – it connects Canada to Europe and vice versa, and it provides some multilateral netting to make the elephant to the south a bit more predictable.[24] NATO is both a tool for Canadian foreign policy and an outcome. Through it, Canada can and does exert influence; without it, Canada would have limited relevance to Europe. Participating in NATO makes Canada relevant not just to the British but also to the Dutch, the French, the Danes, and others who participate in its missions.

Perhaps more important, supporting NATO means helping keep the United States enmeshed in a multilateral military organization. Canada was reminded in 2003 (with the US invasion of Iraq) that a unilateral United States is a difficult neighbour and partner. Smaller countries are always at a disadvantage in working bilaterally with much more powerful countries. Working through institutions that give formal equality, if not always equality in practice, gives Canada equal standing to the United States. While the United States can still make its own choices, as long as it values NATO, it has to take into account the preferences of its members, including Canada. Thus, Canada has always had a strong interest in supporting this organization, and Canadian leaders, including Paul Martin, saw the effort in Afghanistan as part of this long-term pattern and interest. "The prime minister felt that Canada, as a member of NATO, had an obligation to stand with the alliance in Afghanistan, but his interest in Afghanistan ended there."[25] This quote applied to every other country operating in Afghanistan – they were there to support NATO and the United States, and they did not have intrinsic interests in Afghanistan.

As a result of this desire to support NATO and enhance its position,[26] Canada insisted that NATO take over the original ad hoc ISAF effort when Canada agreed to run it in 2003–4 – Hillier's year as commander of ISAF.[27] Likewise, Canada wanted NATO to spread throughout the country, and so Bill Graham, the foreign minister and then defence minister, viewed Canada's role in southern Afghanistan as being aimed at forcing NATO to cover the south.[28] As the first non-US forces to deploy to RC-S, the Canadians played a very important role in setting the stage for the British and

Dutch deployments, with the CF venturing beyond Kandahar to Helmand and Uruzgan.[29]

Making a Difference Is Hard Work

Paul Martin picked Rick Hillier to be CDS not because he was the most senior and next in line (he was not) but because they shared views on the role of the CF in Canadian foreign policy. Martin said that "his views and mine coincided to a fare-thee-well."[30] Specifically, instead of distributing small numbers of troops to various UN and NATO missions so that the Canadian flag would appear all across various maps, Martin and Hillier wanted to concentrate the CF deployments to make a difference and to exert leadership.[31] In Bosnia, Canadian officers had not been invited to the big meetings where the future of the mission was to be decided.[32]

Once the choice was defined as either going to Kandahar and working with the United States, the British, and the Dutch or working in the Italian sector in a remote part of Afghanistan, either Chaghcharan or Herat, the choice that fit with Martin's larger preferences about making a visible difference was Kandahar. It was going to be one of the most important provinces in the country given its history as the homeland of the Taliban, its proximity to Pakistan, the size of its population, and its location in between the British, Dutch, and American sectors of Helmand, Uruzgan, and Zabul, respectively. CIDA, when comparing Kandahar and Herat, found a far greater need in the former as many non-governmental organizations (NGOs) and international agencies were already working in the latter.[33] Chaghcharan ultimately became a Lithuanian responsibility and made little news over the course of the mission. Herat became an American effort, with more visibility than Chaghcharan but still far less than Kandahar.

Kandahar also fit key military interests. It was not only the province in which the Canadians were to be located but also the location of the major airbase in the southern part of Afghanistan. This meant that assistance by plane or helicopter was nearby, that a major medical facility was close, that the commanders of RC-S were near, and that logistics would be easier to finesse since Canadian C-17s could land next to the Canadian base, which was within the Kandahar Air Field (KAF). Chaghcharan was far more remote, with limited access in winter; if anything were to go awry, help would be far away.

Less obvious but perhaps as or even more important, countries in NATO that have worked together in the past like to work together again. Each country has distinct ways of operating, including its own rules of engagement; its own tactics, techniques, and procedures; nationally specific restrictions; and so on. If one is not familiar with a partner's way of military operations, then confusion can happen before, during, and after a battle, presenting significant dangers.[34] Canada had operated in the same sector of Bosnia as the Dutch and the British and had frequently exercised and had exchanges with the Americans. These countries were known quantities, and Canadian officers could anticipate how each would behave on the battlefield. The same was not true for the Italians, with whom the Canadians had very little military experience. It does not mean that there was no friction with the British, the Dutch, or the Americans, but there was certainly less than would have existed with the Italians.

It is not only how the Italians operated – they did not engage in offensive operations, nor did they allow Afghans on their helicopters – but with what equipment. The Italians brought only a handful of helicopters to facilitate movement throughout one-quarter of the country, as the Germans did in a different fourth of Afghanistan. The Americans and British brought far more than that. Even if they could not always provide a ride and often complained when the Canadians asked, the Canadians could and did count on them to show up, especially in emergency situations. It is hard to imagine the CF having as much trust in the Italian contingent.

The reality that some countries operated differently than others – in terms of where they served or how they were restricted – meant that NATO changed somewhat its standard procedures for allocating influence and authority. Important positions have always been distributed based on the size of a country's commitment, with the "Flag to Post" exercise of allotting positions for generals and admirals largely based on size of contingent. In Afghanistan, however, it was not only how big a contingent a country sent but what it was willing to do. Because Canada sent a sizeable force to a dangerous region *and* was willing to move out of its sector to help out NATO partners in neighbouring areas (the British, the Americans, the Dutch, and the Australians), it enjoyed much more influence than the larger German and Italian contingents in Kabul and throughout the NATO chain of command.

Why Not a Token Contribution?

One question remains before concluding this chapter – why not do less? Perhaps attendance in Afghanistan was required of all NATO members, but some showed up in only the most token commitments. For much of the mission, for example, Greece had a total of 15 or so soldiers in Afghanistan despite having one of the largest armies in NATO and being one of the few NATO countries to spend more than 2 per cent of GDP on defence. Canada could have chosen to show up and do little more. The answer, in short, is that the arguments about the "where" also had implications for the "how much." Canada's basic tendency, repeated in mission after mission, from Bosnia to Kosovo to Afghanistan to Libya and now to Iraq, is to do at least as much as the average NATO country. Canada may free-ride when it comes to spending on defence but not when it comes to actual deployments. Supporting the alliance meant showing up in Kandahar and showing up with enough personnel and "kit" to be largely but not entirely self-sufficient. To make a difference in one spot, both Hillier's and Martin's avowed aspiration, meant having not just a token contingent behind the wire but also the full array of NATO effort – a PRT, providing mentors (OMLTs), and a battle group.

Drawing Lessons from the Big Decision

The irony of Paul Martin's protests about the course of the mission is that the high level of violence in Kandahar actually gave Canada far greater visibility in international affairs than it had enjoyed in some time. That Kandahar became a focal point in the insurgency and counter-insurgency made Canada's effort more costly but also more highly valued by alliance partners. From the standpoint of the original objective, the mission "worked." To be clear, Canada did not go into Afghanistan for the sake of the Afghans but to better position itself in international affairs: to solidify relations with the United States, to improve its position within NATO and support the alliance at a critical time, and to visibly make a difference. Of course, when Martin and the Liberals lost the 2006 election and moved into Opposition, they had to criticize the mission because they opposed the government. But oppose the mission that they had initiated? I consider this topic in subsequent chapters.

Before moving on, we need to consider what we can learn from both the Kandahar decision and the debate about it in order to understand how Canada carries out foreign policy. The decision was certainly controversial, which is striking given how little choice Canada really had. This is not to say that Canada was slow to act but rather that the decision was, for all intents and purposes, inevitable. Every member of NATO was setting up shop in Afghanistan somewhere. Canada's military, as we shall see later, was far more up to the task of being in a highly kinetic area than most of the rest of NATO. Canada also had some history in the area, having deployed to Kandahar in 2002. And Canada had a relatively new government striving to make the country more relevant in international affairs, and Kandahar was more important and more visible than most other parts of Afghanistan.

The odd thing is that the decision to go to Kandahar, despite the criticism that it has drawn since then, was, from the standpoint of process, a good one. While there was certainly a dose of wishful thinking involved, the various actors understood that there were significant risks involved. They may have selected the less pessimistic intelligence reports (there were conflicting estimates of how strong the insurgency was), but they took seriously the reality that Kandahar was not Kabul, that it would not be peacekeeping but combat. After the decision was made, Hillier did a "body bag" tour of Canada, informing the public that this new mission was going to be bloody but worth it.[35] All of the relevant actors in Canada's foreign policy process had their say, and the prime minister seriously deliberated. This was not a flippant decision or one based on deceit or mismanagement. The myth that Hillier hoodwinked Paul Martin is untenable and insulting to everyone involved, even if it facilitated the retrospective Liberal opposition to the war.

The extent of official deliberation in Canada becomes even clearer when it is contrasted with the decision of the United States to invade Iraq. President Bush, Vice President Cheney, and Secretary of Defense Rumsfeld marginalized the voices of opposition, including the secretary of state, when making the decision to invade Iraq, and they "gamed" the intelligence used to justify the war. We still do not know who was responsible for disbanding the Iraqi military: Rumsfeld or Paul (Jerry) Bremer, who ran the occupation. In Canada, we know who made the decision to deploy to Kandahar (the prime minister, with the support of Cabinet), we know who advised the prime minister, and we know that the prime minister took the decision seriously.[36] Yes, the military, represented by General Rick Hillier, favoured it, but so did much of DFAIT, given the international interests at stake in Washington, Brussels, and Kabul, and so did the foreign policy community.

The debate about the decision does a great disservice not only to those who were at the key meetings but also to Canadians' understanding of their political system. Are Canada's civilian leaders such amateurs that they can be easily manipulated by an "Americanized" military? If this were the case, it would truly be a crisis in Canadian civil-military relations – that civilians are naive or foolish, that the military has ulterior motives, and that the military wins these contests for the conduct of Canadian foreign policy.

One of the key themes in the coverage of the war was that Canadians were confused by Afghanistan. One source of this confusion has been the Liberals' effort to deny responsibility, and the book written by Stein and former Liberal adviser Lang plays a key role in this. Recasting the Kandahar decision means that Canadians are less likely to evaluate it on its original terms – the price of being involved in international affairs, the cost of being a part of NATO and a partner of the United States, and the premium for making a difference in the world. One can argue whether such goals were worth more than 160 Canadian lives and billions of dollars, but that is a more productive and a more mature conversation to have than whether Hillier and the CF were too tied to the United States and too willing to lie to the prime minister.

The key implications of this chapter for understanding Canada today and into the future are these:

- The Kandahar decision shows that the Canadian political system can make the hard decisions necessary in a challenging international environment.
- The debate about the decision shows that the various parties are not sufficiently mature to take responsibility when the decisions have consequences.[37]

In the next chapter, I address the dynamics of minority government at war: that the requirements of Opposition gave the Liberals incentives to revise their views on Afghanistan; how the new Conservative government handled the responsibilities of the mission, including extending it; and the longer-term implications of these processes.

chapter four

The Power of Minority Government: Manipulating the Confused and Those Who Cannot Cooperate

Perhaps one of the most confounding elements of the entire Canadian experience with the Afghanistan mission is that it largely overlapped with a series of minority governments. Unlike New Zealand and many European countries, Canada has rarely experienced minority government and practically none while at war.[1] The Liberal Party, which was in power when the Kandahar decision was made, began opposing that same mission once it lost power yet still had enough MPs voting to extend it. Parliamentary votes in 2006 and 2008 to extend the mission proved most confusing, creating a belief that the prime minister of Canada needed parliamentary approval to deploy troops into harm's way.[2] The prime minister is empowered to send Canadian forces into harm's way without parliamentary votes, but minority government provided both *constraints* and *opportunities* that led to the holding of such votes. These votes did much to shape media coverage and public perception of the mission and, in part, created the view that deployments of the CF required parliamentary votes.

While minority government coexisted with the Afghanistan conflict from 2004 to 2011, the critical period was 2007–8, when Stephen Harper sought to extend the mission, which otherwise would have ended in 2009. To gain enough support from the Liberals, Harper created a commission to study the Afghanistan effort, led by former Liberal Cabinet minister John Manley. The Manley Panel and the subsequent renewal process influenced politics at home and the mission overseas, including setting an end date to the Kandahar mission despite the panel's recommendation. The process had many effects, including, at least from Harper's perspective, largely ending debate about the mission. From 2008 on, Harper was able to hide from the mission, with some help from the Liberals, who also sought to dodge responsibility, as I document below.

Seeing as it was such a crucial period, a closer look at 2007–8 can do much to suggest lessons about how Canada may operate in the future, with or without minority government complicating the politics. In this chapter, I first consider the context of Liberal opposition and the dilemmas Harper faced. I then consider the many different purposes that the Manley Panel served. I move on to consider what the panel recommended and how its recommendations were shaped by parliamentary politics. I will save the impact of the Manley Panel on the mission in Kandahar for the discussion of WG in Chapter 6.

Minority Support and the Manley Panel

When Stephen Harper became prime minister in January 2006, he faced a much tougher challenge than his predecessor, Paul Martin. Even though he had had a hung Parliament, Martin could count on Conservative support for the Afghanistan mission; therefore, he did not bother to submit the initial Kandahar deployment to a vote. Harper did not have a majority of seats in Parliament either, and the Liberals, who had started the Afghanistan mission, soon became divided over it. Thus, Harper faced the possibility of confidence votes, a political reality complicated by his commitment to the idea of holding votes for foreign deployments.[3] While Harper may have been able to dodge that commitment if he had had a majority of seats, he could not while governing with only a plurality.

The first test came in the spring of 2006, when a decision had to be made to extend the mission beyond 2007, the initial commitment made by Paul Martin. Harper called for an emergency debate, limited to six hours, to push through an extension to 2009.[4] The vote was close as the Bloc Québécois and the New Democratic Party (NDP) voted against the extension, while Bill Graham (who had been defence minister when the original decision was made) allowed the Liberals to vote as they saw fit. Only 30 Liberals out of 103 joined the Conservatives. Liberal opposition only strengthened when Bill Graham's interim leadership ended and he was replaced by Stéphane Dion, who had voted against the mission.[5]

Thus, the first extension set the stage for the next extension vote in 2008. It was clear that unless Harper did something to once again divide the Liberals,[6] either the extension vote would not pass, and Canada would be put in the embarrassing position of pulling its troops off the battlefield earlier than the rest of its allies, or Harper would have to backtrack on his party's commitment to taking such votes seriously.[7] Another way to look at this is that the 2006 vote had given Harper a chance to divide the Liberals,[8] and the 2008 extension vote would serve as a similar opportunity to put the Liberals in a difficult spot.

Harper asked John Manley, a former Liberal leader and deputy prime minister, to form a commission (hereafter referred to as the Manley Panel) to evaluate the state of the mission and make recommendations.

The Manley Panel undertook hundreds of interviews; travelled to Afghanistan; and met with Afghans, ISAF officers, and many others. It rejected all four options that Harper gave it in its terms of reference: train the Afghan army and police, with a phased withdrawal starting in 2009; continue to carry out development and governance while another country provides security; shift to some other spot in Afghanistan; or pull out entirely but leave a modest number of forces to provide security for any Canadian civilians who stay.[9]

Instead, the panel recommended that as long as certain conditions were met, the CF should maintain its responsibilities in Kandahar, "including its combat role, but with increasing emphasis on training the Afghan National Security Forces."[10] The recommendation did not include a deadline as the panel found that there was no rationale for any specific deadline.[11] The conditions did include more NATO help in the province (one battle group), more helicopters, and drones. The panel also recommended that Canada change how it did business in Afghanistan, placing a greater focus on bilateral assistance to those in Kandahar, making clearer assessments of progress, and giving "franker and more frequent reporting" to the Canadian public, with "greater emphasis to the diplomatic and reconstruction efforts."[12] Because of frustration with how the various efforts had failed to be integrated, the Manley Report urged:

> These efforts should be led by the Prime Minister, supported by a special cabinet committee and by a single task force directing the activities of all departments and agencies. The objective is to ensure better balance, tighter coordination and more systematic evaluation of Canada's contributions.[13]

Implications of the Manley Panel

The Manley Report gave nearly everyone involved something they wanted.[14] Given their complaints that the mission was too heavily weighted towards combat, with too little focus on governance and development, the Liberals found much to like in the panel's recommendations. Whether Harper believed in governance and development in Afghanistan or not, the Manley Panel and the extension vote compelled a greater Whole of Government effort by placing more emphasis and attention on the non-military side of things. How this actually played out proved to be more complex (see Chapter 6).

More important, though, the Liberals got a deadline. The Manley Panel had explicitly avoided setting a deadline, arguing that the mission should be studied a few years down the road to see what should be done. "Ending Canada's military contribution in Kandahar is therefore *not a matter of setting artificial deadlines in time*. It is a matter of making real progress in the context of events on the ground."[15] But having a deadline was the one real compromise that had been embedded in the parliamentary motion of 2008 that supported the extension of the mission – that Canadian forces would be leaving Kandahar in July of 2011. This directly contradicted the Manley Panel's recommendation. The Liberals had pushed for a deadline and got it, but it eventually worked in Stephen Harper's favour.[16]

As a result of the shift in focus towards governance and development resulting from the Manley Report, and in response to the criticisms about civilian coordination on the ground, a new position was created: the Representative of Canada in Kandahar, otherwise known as the RoCK. It was responsible for not just the DFAIT effort in Kandahar but also the entire civilian effort in the province: DFAIT, CIDA, the Royal Canadian Mounted Police (RCMP), the Department of Public Safety, the Correctional Service of Canada (CSC), etc. Indeed, the RoCK was to be seen as being coequal with the CF commander of the troops in the province. Elissa Golberg of DFAIT, and formerly of the Manley Panel, was the first person to hold this position. At the same time, the Afghanistan Task Force was created in Ottawa, situated within the Privy Council Office and headed by a deputy minister, first David Mulroney and then Greta Bossenmaier, both DFAIT veterans; the former had played a role on the Manley Panel. With these appointments, DFAIT gained significant influence.

The CF gained a lot from the Manley process as well. The renewal vote, with the one battle group condition, compelled NATO to provide more help, even though, as we have established, Canada was never really alone in Kandahar. As a result of this process and the need to get a vote passed, the United States ultimately committed a battalion to serve under Canadian command in the province.[17] This preceded Obama's surge by two years. The CF also won a government commitment to provide helicopters and drones, both aimed at reducing casualties by avoiding and monitoring the dangerous roads that had cost many Canadian lives.[18]

Stephen Harper received the political cover necessary to convince enough Liberals to vote for an extension. Some have argued off the record that the Manley Panel's big bonus for Harper was to enhance civilian control of the military; by creating a key position, to be held by Mulroney, to coordinate the entire effort, it gave Harper a more direct means by which to control the military. (I return to this point in Chapter 6.) The key here is that the Manley Report gave Harper a wedge to divide the Liberals, which was good in itself as well as for extending the mission. Indeed, some would argue that by submitting this extension to Parliament, Harper was able to "launder" the mission, obscuring who was ultimately accountable for it.[19]

Confused Accountability: Harper Hides

For Stephen Harper, the Manley Panel and the second extension vote of 2008 did more than just help extend the mission. It meant sharing responsibility for the mission with the Liberals so that the Liberals could not really run on the Afghanistan issue in subsequent elections. Moreover, the 2011 deadline provided a tremendous service to Harper as any and all questions about the future of the mission could be answered by reference to Parliament's 2011 deadline. Harper repeatedly said that there would be only enough troops left after 2011 to guard the Canadian embassy. As it turned out, he shifted his stance abruptly in late 2010, sending a heavily restricted training mission to Kabul (and elsewhere but not Kandahar). In the interim, the vote and its deadline ended the discussions in Ottawa about the fate of the mission, which meant that the opposition and the media had to turn elsewhere (to the issue of detainees, discussed in Chapter 5). What the vote and the deadline really did was give Harper a tool to deflect questions about the mission.

Despite Harper's initial enthusiasm for the mission, it presented him with a variety of problems that reduced his interest. For example, the Afghan mission enhanced the power of the CF, especially that of General Rick Hillier, to the point where it seemed that the military was setting policy rather than the government. Given Harper's tendency towards centralizing power in his office, the ascent of Hillier was quite a problem.

A second problem was Quebec, where opposition to the mission was much stronger than in the rest of Canada, making it harder for the Conservatives to gain seats in that province.[20] Politically, then, it was efficacious for Harper to put the mission as far in the background as possible.

A third problem was that a highly kinetic and visible mission in Afghanistan provided a critical threat to one of Harper's key strategies: controlling the messaging of the Canadian government. There are bountiful examples of Harper's message-management tendencies, including banning journalists from hotels where the Conservative caucus was meeting, setting up an elaborate process to vet all public statements, cancelling events due to delays in vetting, and more.[21] Over the course of the mission, the only actors that had wide discretion to speak to the media were the troops on the ground in Kandahar. The talking points of DFAIT and CIDA were apparently reviewed at the highest levels of government; even senior people in the Public Relations branch of the Department of National Defence (DND) complained of intense restrictions.[22] Silencing the CF in Afghanistan, however, was simply impossible. The reality of embedding journalists within 2,000 (or more) soldiers, combined with a pre-existing policy that any member of the CF could talk to the media,[23] meant that Harper could not control the messaging of the mission as much as he might have liked. It was politically impossible to demand that soldiers not talk to the media and also impossible to enforce.

Still, Harper could try to minimize the frequency with which the issue appeared in the media by simply talking about it less often. Figure 4.1 below illustrates this trend quite well, showing that in 2008, Harper significantly cut back on speaking about Afghanistan in public, to the press, and in Parliament.[24]

The number of times Harper spoke about the Afghanistan mission sharply declined in and after 2008. The Promote line in the figure records the number of appearances he made to promote the effort. The remaining appearances (included in the Total line) reflect his public reaction to events, such as casualties in Afghanistan or meetings with foreign officials; meeting with the troops; and relatively modest or token mentions of the mission. This simple figure illustrates a few key points but clearly shows that Harper dramatically cut back efforts to promote the mission after 2007. However, perhaps a better indicator of message management at work is that he stopped responding to events at all, as Figure 4.2 below indicates.

Figure 4.1: Harper's Mentions of Afghanistan, 2006–12

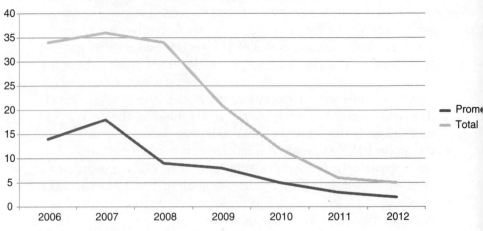

While events can be seen as compelling a leader to talk about an effort, it seems to be the case that either Afghanistan became much less compelling around this time or Harper did not feel compelled to speak publicly about it. Given that there was another prison break in 2011 and Canadians kept killing and being killed in Kandahar until the last few months of the mission, it seems to be the case that Harper chose not to react publicly.

Did it work? I consider this at greater length in Chapter 8, but one indicator is whether Canadians asked questions about it. Using Google Trends, one can find patterns of searches for various terms. After I performed a search using "Harper" and "Afghanistan," Google Trends produced Figure 4.3 below.[25]

Canadians searched for Harper's stance on Afghanistan using Google most intensely in 2006, with declining interest in 2008 and further declines after that. This is modest evidence, of course, and I will examine the various polls in Chapter 8. Nevertheless, Figure 4.3 still suggests that Canadians became less curious about Harper and Afghanistan at about the same time he started avoiding public mentions of the mission.

Again, having a set endpoint for the Kandahar mission was politically very useful to Stephen Harper, providing a convenient response to probing questions about its progress. This effectively

Figure 4.2: Harper's Mentions of Afghanistan, 2006–12, by Type

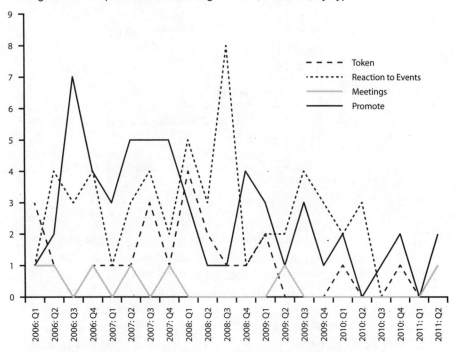

removed Afghanistan as a campaign issue in 2008 and 2011, much to the Conservatives' benefit. The Liberals were divided on the issue, as explained earlier, and thus compromised. And while the NDP and the Bloc pushed for a quicker withdrawal in 2008, the Manley Report and the parliamentary vote had settled the matter. Harper simply responded to the NDP and Bloc by indicating that the withdrawal would happen in 2011 and anything sooner would be irresponsible. As a result, the elections turned on other issues, and the parties and media were left to cover other stories.

A Failure to Cooperate: The Lame Opposition

Minority governments are minority governments for a reason: the opposition parties fail to cooperate enough to form a coalition that

Figure 4.3: Searching for Harper's Stance on Afghanistan

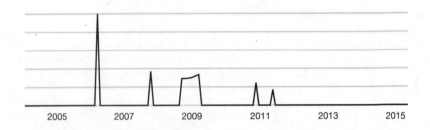

Source: Google Trends. Google and the Google logo are registered trademarks of Google Inc., used with permission.

can govern. While coalitions are apparently anathema in Canada, the three opposition parties could have cooperated at any time to compel the government to change its policies or lose a vote of confidence. Given that two of the parties wanted to see the mission end as soon as possible, it is somewhat surprising that Stephen Harper was able to maintain the Kandahar mission until 2011 given that the third party, the Liberals, was not very fond of the mission that they had started.

The NDP opposed the extensions in 2006 and 2008. In 2006, leader Jack Layton argued, "The New Democrats have not written a blank cheque so that this government, or any other government, can drag Canada still farther into war, so that it can remove us farther from our role as international peacekeepers."[26] In 2008, this stance was clearer still, demanding an immediate withdrawal as the war was a "mistake."[27] Strangely enough, the NDP did not support a Liberal motion to end the mission in 2009, arguing that they preferred the mission to end immediately. This could be seen as an artful dodge to avoid an election when the NDP was not ready.[28]

Politically, the NDP had a very easy decision to make for each vote. The two mainstream parties, the Conservatives and Liberals, were implicated in the war, so opposing the war could distinguish the party and appeal to MPs of those parties who were opposed to Canada's involvement. Moreover, this position played well with the pacifists in the NDP's base. It was a position that could appeal beyond the party without losing support within it; for example, the appeals to Canada's peacekeeping history would play to Liberal voters' nostalgia for a soft-power past. The 2006 NDP election platform promised to "reorient Canada's defence procurement to support the priorities of peacekeeping, peacemaking, humanitarian and environmental support operations."[29]

The Bloc Québécois opposed the mission in the 2006 election. Like the NDP, the Bloc had a significant pacifist constituency. While Quebec pacifism is perhaps overstated, many Quebeckers tend not to be enthusiastic about the use of force, especially when it seems to be at the behest of the United States.[30] The first vote allowed the Bloc to take a strong stance against the Conservatives for disrespecting Parliament, given the rushed vote.

In his typical fashion, the Prime Minister has decided to call a rushed vote on extending Canada's military commitment. It was, "There will be a vote or I will decide without a vote." That is why we agreed to have a vote. However, just because we agreed to have a vote does not mean we will vote absolutely in favour. That is not what democracy is all about. By rushing matters, the Prime Minister is being irresponsible, in my opinion. This shows a lack of respect for the House of Commons, parliamentarians and the public. It is offensive.[31]

Like the NDP, the Bloc could use the vote in 2008 to attack both the Conservatives and the Liberals.

As is now policy here in the House of Commons, the Conservatives have twisted the mission.... This mission was supposed to be focused on diplomacy and development, but that is no longer true. It is almost entirely a defence mission. For a whole year the Liberal Party carried the standard for those who wanted to end the operations in February 2009 but now they have surrendered and gone over to the Conservatives. That is terribly disappointing.[32]

Politically, then, the NDP and the Bloc achieved a win-win: they could oppose policies that their bases did not like *and* criticize both the Conservatives and the Liberals. On the other hand, this opposition had key consequences. While the two parties became quite distinct from their larger counterparts, the line between them was obscured. Given that they were both pursuing voters in Quebec, their stances did not set the two parties apart from each other. This ultimately proved to be more problematic for the Bloc in 2011 than the NDP.

The Liberals were consistently inconsistent throughout the mission. Not only were they ambivalent about their stance on the mission, but they were also quite divided over whether to cooperate with the opposing parties or not. In 2008, an effort was made to form a coalition between the NDP and the Liberals, with the Bloc's support, but it failed.[33] The focus of this effort was not Afghanistan but the budget that the Conservatives had tabled; even so, it shows how difficult it is to form coalitions in Canada, something that is truly exceptional. Harper was able to attack the proposed coalition by tying the Liberals to the Bloc. "At a time like this, a coalition with the separatists cannot help Canada."[34] This situation, combined with the prorogation of Parliament and a leadership crisis within the Liberal Party, quashed the one attempt to counter the minority Conservative government by means of a coalition.

A key constraint during this time frame was that the opposition parties generally did not want another election – the polls indicated that they would lose.[35] So they were constrained as they could not agree to bring down the government with a vote of no confidence in the Afghanistan mission. Ultimately, the inability of the various opposition parties to cooperate with each other limited their impact, and that of Parliament, on the mission.[36]

Conclusions

Minority government may mean more power, not less. Ineffective opposition plus some selective buy-in means less accountability. Stephen Harper played the opposition quite well, dividing the Liberals when he needed to so that the extension votes could pass. By garnering just enough support, he was able to implicate the

Liberals in the war effort. And he was able to launder the mission so that the government appeared less accountable. While one can imagine how shared responsibility might lead to mutual accountability, in practice, as mastered by Harper, it meant that no party was really held accountable for the success or failure of the Afghanistan mission.

Whether one is impressed by Harper depends on whether one values political tenacity, strategy, and leadership. He managed to stay in power and eventually gain a majority government in the 2011 election. However, he largely abdicated responsibility for the most costly Canadian military effort since Korea. Instead of standing in front of the mission, he adapted and evaded it, using the parliamentary motion of 2008 as a shield. The NATO commitment, the drain on Canada's budget, the ramp ceremonies, and the procession of coffins coming home all weighed heavily on the Canadian government, just as they did on the governments of the other members of NATO. Some politicians took ownership, such as those in Denmark, which propped up public support for the mission for a longer time. Others, such as Harper, tried to escape responsibility.

At the same time, the opposition parties squandered opportunities to hold the Conservatives accountable. The Liberals were not united in their stance on the mission. The NDP and the Bloc could each take a stance, but the three parties could not cooperate to impose their will on the government. It is true that the Liberals got an end date of 2011 and may have compelled Harper to take the civilian side of the mission more seriously. However, he had his own reasons for keeping the deadline and for doing more WG.

Because the question of extending the Kandahar mission was settled with the 2008 parliamentary motion, the opposition parties had to focus elsewhere if they wanted to use Afghanistan to make the government look bad. The detainee issue fit the bill, even though the parties could have asked more challenging questions about the mission and what was being accomplished.

The irony of minority governments is a modification of the classic Spider-Man aphorism: that with great power comes great responsibility. Instead, minority government can mean both *more power* and *less responsibility*.[37] The Conservatives and the Liberals both underperformed in the case of the Afghanistan mission. The Liberals tried to duck responsibility for a mission they had started by arguing that "the job of the opposition is to oppose."[38] Ultimately, while it is hard to find direct evidence through polls, I can only believe that this reversal cost them much credibility and that their lack of unity caused the Liberals to forfeit the mantle of the voice of reason in Canadian foreign policy.[39] Again, Harper was able to stay in power but at the cost of letting the mission go adrift.

chapter five

The Problematic Parliament: Detainees, Information Asymmetries, and a Misplaced Focus

A few years ago, I asked Claude Bachand, defence critic for the Bloc Québécois, what he knew of the rules of engagement followed by the CF, and he said that he did not know.[1] Why not? Because he did not possess a security clearance, which meant that Canadian generals would tell him that they could not answer his questions. This surprised me greatly as I grew up in the United States, where, for all of its flaws, it allows representatives and senators serving on relevant committees to have security clearances, which allow them to ask probing questions and see classified documents. Paul Martin, when I interviewed him about the larger mission, responded to my questions on this matter by insisting that I was looking at the wrong cases to compare – that British-style systems do oversight differently than the American Congress.[2] Indeed, he argued that given the lack of expertise and the frequent turnover on the defence and similar committees, it would not be feasible to empower defence committee members with security clearances.

Further investigation revealed that Canadian MPs and senators do not see their role as being overseers but rather holding the minister to account.[3] The problem is this: how does one hold a minister accountable if one does not know key aspects of what is going on? How does one know the right questions to ask if one has little context? How can one ask questions during Question Period when the matters are related to classified operations or information? This was not at all just a matter of theory during the Afghanistan mission as a critical aspect of the detainee issue was how to give parliamentarians the information they needed.

The information problem represented one of two key dynamics that the detainee controversy demonstrated, as we see below; the second was Parliament's misplaced focus. Given the Somalia episode's impact on the CF and Canadian politics,[4] it is not surprising that detainees would be a subject of some concern in Ottawa. That approximately two-thirds of the Question Period sessions that focused on Afghanistan addressed the issue of detention is instructive.[5] This chapter uses the detainee issue to understand the limitations of Canada's Parliament when it comes to foreign deployments: that the MPs lacked the power, the expertise, and the interest to engage in serious accounting of the Afghanistan effort. Instead, they focused on an issue that had some potential to explode but was hardly pivotal on the ground in Afghanistan and not at all unique to those countries engaged in the mission.

Below, I first consider the Canadian controversy regarding detainees in Afghanistan. I then consider two issues: the *information problem* – and how workarounds were developed – and the *focus problem* – that Parliament was looking in the wrong place. In the case of the information problem, when I asked my interviewees whether Canada's parliamentarians preferred to be ignorant critics or informed overseers, the answer was usually the former. In the case of Afghanistan, the answer is pretty clear as the detainee investigation produced far more heat than light.

The Detainee Problem

Whenever Canada and other countries take part in a multilateral military mission, including peacekeeping operations, there is always the issue of how to handle those individuals who are detained. With perhaps only one exception, countries do not build long-term imprisonment facilities in the countries in which they intervene. That one exception, of course, is the United States. In Kosovo, for instance, NATO forces could deliver their detainees to the American facility – Camp Bondsteel. Afghanistan exacerbated this challenge in at least three ways.

1. The type of mission – COIN – meant that more individuals would be detained.
2. The existing set of standards – Afghanistan's history of prisoner treatment – was a severe mismatch with Canadian norms (and those of the other NATO members).
3. The definition of the mission – to support the development of a self-sustaining, sovereign Afghanistan – meant that the outsiders would be turning over captured Afghans to the Afghan government.

An additional development complicated things further: the United States had lost its role as the detainer of last resort. In prior missions, handing over detainees to the Americans was relatively unproblematic. However, the use of torture in various American detention facilities, but especially Abu Ghraib and Guantanamo Bay, as well as rendition (sending detainees to their home countries, where they could be tortured), made it politically impossible for NATO members and partners to hand over their detainees to American custody.[6]

Not Just a Canadian Problem

All of the allies faced a serious problem: they could not hold on to detainees for long, so they had to turn them over to the Afghan authorities, who had a history of abusing their detainees. Each country ultimately developed its own bilateral deal with the Afghans for how their prisoners were to be treated and monitored.

Denmark, for instance, developed a detailed legal framework that sought to ensure that detainees would not be abused once they were handed over to Afghan authorities.[7] However, this was not entirely unproblematic. Working with the Afghans in Helmand raised concerns that Danish forces might become complicit in abuses. This helps to explain why the Danes were reluctant to embed as trainers in Afghan units – it was not so much that they were not willing to engage in risky combat but that they did not want to work alongside the ANA for fear of being present when abuses of detainees took place.[8]

The Netherlands, as lead nation in Uruzgan, had to hold onto prisoners for at least a while. It built a prison that was supposed to handle 10 or so detainees but had to expand it. It then developed a policy similar to the rest of NATO – hand over to the Afghan authorities within 96 hours or release.[9] In reality, it sometimes held detainees over 96 hours as it was often difficult to book planes to transport prisoners to Kabul. After handing over, a Dutch representative would visit the prisoners every month. As the number of transferred detainees accumulated over time, this process became more challenging. Again, a bilateral deal was negotiated to cover the transfer of detainees and allow visits by Dutch monitors, the Red Cross, and others.[10]

Romania turned over detainees immediately to the Afghan National Police (ANP) or ANA unless they were captured by SOF units, in which case they would be turned over to the United States. The key restriction was that Romanian soldiers could not turn over detainees if the death penalty could be imposed.[11]

Australia's policy was to transfer low-risk detainees to the Afghan authorities and high-risk ones to the Americans. This policy received more attention after all of the coverage of the Canadian detainee story. This led to a series of updates by Defence Minister Stephen Smith on the state of detainee transfers.[12] Transfers were suspended in 2011 after ISAF itself suspended them. A key difference between Australia and Canada is that some Australian troops were accused of abusing prisoners. While most charges were dismissed, a few officers were charged with falsifying documents, and a couple of others were investigated for verbal abuse of detainees.[13]

The United Kingdom, like Canada, faced some serious media attention for its detainee policies. In this case, the stories were driven by lawsuits brought by activists, who argued that Afghan detainees were abused by Afghan authorities after being turned over by the British. While prisoners were then sent to facilities with better reputations,[14] the British government suspended transfers in late 2012 because the chances of abuse were seen as being too high.[15]

This short survey of some of the allies illustrates a basic reality – Afghanistan was a difficult place in which to operate for a variety of reasons, and the outsiders faced common problems. They responded rather similarly – trying to finesse the problem while mostly denying the severity of the situation. The Canadian story is not unique.

How the Canadian Government Handled the Detainee Issue

In the Canadian case, we need to be clear: the CF was not accused of beating detainees, nor was it accused of American-style rendition in cases where its soldiers were present while detainees were being tortured. Still, I should not underplay the dilemmas involved as handing over prisoners knowing that they will be tortured can be a war crime. The focus here is not on whether the CF acted perfectly (I think it largely did the best it could do in a difficult situation) but how Parliament handled the issue as it says much about Parliament's limits.

One of the most striking aspects of the detainee controversy was how clear things were in Kandahar and how opaque they became in Ottawa. During a week-long tour to Kabul and Kandahar in late 2007 organized by NATO and DND, I had a chance to see Canada's temporary detainment facility and chat with the Canadian military police there. The facility consisted mostly of fencing, which kept prisoners apart and under a bit of cover, but the detainees were still exposed to the elements. The military police with whom we spoke discussed the intake process, including taking photographs to confirm the condition of the prisoners as they were received, and said that they would be transferred ordinarily within 96 hours to Afghan authorities. Yet the military police also told us that at the time that the handovers were suspended, there had been reports of prisoners being abused after being transferred. In short, the CF seemed to be doing its best in a difficult circumstance.

In Ottawa, the situation was seen to be quite different. The government denied that there was much of a problem despite widespread reports of Afghan authorities torturing and even "disappearing" those who had been turned over by members of the international community. General Rick Hillier had signed an agreement with Afghan authorities in December 2005 to make sure that prisoners would be treated according to the Geneva conventions,[16] but the agreement did not ensure sufficient monitoring. The hope was that the International Committee of the Red Cross would monitor the prisoners, but it did not seem to agree to the role for which the Canadians had hoped. In May 2007, a different agreement was developed that would improve monitoring while also increasing Canadian training of corrections officers in Kandahar. In between, Canadian capacity to monitor was limited as the death of Glyn Berry in January 2006 led to a halt in Canadian civilian efforts in Kandahar, and then, only gradually, were there enough civilians to go outside the wire to monitor the prisons.[17]

While reports filtered back that prisoners were being abused, the government denied it, saying that while abuses may have occurred, there was no evidence that those who had previously been in Canadian custody were abused after being transferred. This argument did not seem to be entirely persuasive and perhaps cut things too finely, and the opposition parties and human rights groups attacked the government and accused it of lying. The combination of newspaper reporting, especially by Graeme Smith, and whistleblowing by DFAIT's Richard Colvin, shone the spotlight on the issue.[18]

Parliament's Information Problem

The issue drew Parliament's attention in a big way, as we will see below. However, MPs could do little more than complain about what they read in the newspapers as they did not have access to the government documents related to the issue. When they sought these documents, the Harper government resisted, claiming that these were sensitive materials and they should not be released to the public unless they were heavily redacted.[19] The House of Commons finally issued an order in December 2009 for the government to produce the materials related to the detainee file, and the Speaker ruled in April 2010 that the House could ask for the documents. This might suggest that the system worked as Parliament compelled the government to give it the information it sought, but only if we use a low threshold for what counts as "working" since the process took far longer than it should have, produced only limited access, and was only possible due to minority government.

The order led to a memorandum of understanding between Stephen Harper and the leaders of two of the opposition parties (Michael Ignatieff of the Liberals and Gilles Duceppe of the Bloc Québécois), which specified a procedure by which an ad hoc committee would be formed that would have limited access to the documents.[20] This agreement gave the parliamentarians selected to serve on the committee limited security clearances – they could see the documents in a government facility but could take only those notes that they would leave behind in the facility. They were not allowed to disclose what they found, but instead were mainly tasked with recommending which documents should be released and which redactions should be removed. A Panel of Arbiters consisting of three jurists would then decide which documents to release and how, based in part on the recommendations of the committee.

It took a great deal of conflict between the opposition parties and the government to reach this compromise. However, in the end, it did not achieve that much: it created a process that eventually led to only a few documents reaching Parliament: 4,000 out of 40,000, or 10 per cent.[21] And it almost certainly took far longer than if the ad hoc committee had simply had security clearances.[22] As a result, the discussions created far more heat than light. As one senator pointed out to me, parliamentary committees do not have any real budgetary authority (although Parliament itself votes on the budget), unlike those in the United States, so they have no "real hammer" to create pressure or punish agencies that are obstinate or misbehave.[23] On the other hand, the opposition parties could have cooperated to cause the government to fall owing to the confidence convention surrounding money bills, which is a far bigger hammer. Perhaps its bluntness limits its utility.

The Problem of Parliament's Focus

The detainee issue was a serious one, but it still seems strange that it received an overwhelming amount of attention from Parliament compared to the rest of the mission in Kandahar. (See Figure 5.1 below.) It was easy to forget that the CF was doing anything besides transferring detainees, at least if one was paying attention to Question Period.

Figure 5.1 shows that when Afghanistan was a focal point of Question Period during the Kandahar mission, a very significant percentage of time was dedicated to the detainee issue, sometimes almost to the exclusion of all others. This was particularly the case in 2007 and 2010. The problem is that there was far more to the Afghanistan mission and far more to Canada's efforts there than detainees. Here are just some of the issues that could have used a bit more discussion if the job of Parliament is actually to hold the government accountable.

- Did the CF have too few troops to do the job? If so, why?
- How compatible were Canadian values with those that Canada was supporting in Afghanistan? Did it matter? If trade-offs had to be made, what would be the implications of different choices?
- What policies did Canada have to provide benefits to the Canadian civilians (DFAIT, CIDA, etc.) going into harm's way? How did differences between the civilians' benefits and those of the soldiers affect the mission?
- Which agencies of the Canadian government played well with others? Which ones did the worst in WG efforts? Why?
- What were the implications of the particular choices made for the three signature projects (see Chapter 6)?
- Were the quarterly reports to Parliament accurate? Whose voices were diminished or scrubbed out?

Figure 5.1: Question Period, Afghanistan, and Detainees[24]

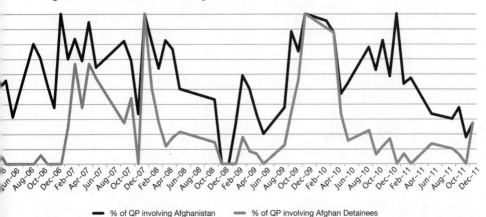

— % of QP involving Afghanistan   — % of QP involving Afghan Detainees

- How did Canada deal with the challenge of focusing on Kandahar when NATO was developing policies for the entire country? That is, what happened when Canadian commanders and civilian officials faced conflicting pressures from Ottawa and Brussels?

Of course, the big question, one that did not receive enough attention in Parliament, was what the Canadian effort in Afghanistan was actually achieving. Indeed, this is a difficult question, but it deserved far more attention than the topic of detainees. Yes, the latter presented some risk of scandal and perhaps accusations about war crimes, but the former was far more important. What were Canadians paying for? What were Canadians risking their lives and their limbs for? This required asking difficult questions, but if the goal was to hold the government accountable, then Parliament should have been focused on holding it to account for the mission itself and not just one highly visible and controversial component.[25]

Perhaps the Liberals did not want to ask these big questions since they were complicit as a result of the votes in 2006 and 2008. However, the NDP and the Bloc could have been asking these questions. Alas, the Martin mantra discussed in Chapter 4 – the duty of the opposition is to oppose – seemed to mean, strangely enough, that the job was not to criticize, at least over non-detainee issues.

The Limited Relevance of Parliament in Civil-Military Relations

If one wants to study Canadian civil-military relations, even during the height of Canada's military efforts, one can probably ignore Parliament.[26] During the Afghanistan mission, the limitations of the institution and those that inhabit it came into sharp relief. It took several years of controversy for a small number of MPs, far smaller than the average defence committee, to gain temporary and highly managed access to documents related to the most important (as measured by Question Period focus) dimension of Canada's most expensive and dangerous mission since the Korean War. In other countries, parliamentarians on defence committees are granted regular and systematic access to the classified information that might inform their views about the status of their country's military endeavours.[27] Officers and officials in such countries know that their feet will be held to the fire if they mislead their legislatures. In Canada, MPs are largely ignorant about the CF and almost always happy to remain so.[28] Some, such as Senator Colin Kenney, rely upon leaks to gain more insight into what is happening,[29] but that is likely to be episodic at best and highly biased much of the time.

If the job of an MP is to hold an office holder accountable, one can do that job well only if one has a decent chance of knowing what the official is and is not doing. If the official to be held accountable is the source of information, there might just be some limits to his or her accountability. Because defence committee members do not possess security clearances, they are largely blind when it comes to what the CF may or may not be doing. And when parliamentarians seek to know more about what the CF is doing, they have a very difficult time when the government is tempted to classify anything and everything. I was told by one staffer of a defence critic that when they wanted to know something about the CF, they called the Pentagon.

Of course, oversight, if empowered, can be problematic if it is used just to attack the government rather than hold it accountable. The quality of oversight over the American military, for example, has varied over time as partisanship often overcomes the responsibilities of representatives and senators to oversee. Given how tightly parties are controlled in Canada,[30] an empowered Parliament may be unlikely to provide that much insight or oversight.[31] Indeed, the behaviour during the Afghanistan mission suggests that an empowered Parliament would still have been distracted by the highly visible but less central stories, such as detainees, rather than those that addressed the mission directly. The potential to accuse the government of war crimes was far more important to the opposing parties than evaluating the mission itself. And for its part, the government, rather than acknowledging a serious problem, denied, denied, and then denied some more, restricting access to information and thus feeding the fire focused on the detainee matter.

While many actors in the Canadian system learned lessons from this conflict and adapted over the course of the decade, we cannot really count Parliament or parliamentarians among them. In the events since the exit from Kandahar, MPs have remained just as irrelevant as before. For instance, Canada deployed CF-18s to Eastern Europe as part of NATO's reassurance effort in the aftermath of Russian aggression in Ukraine, and then it sent trainers to Ukraine itself. This may not be combat, but sending the CF to a country that is at war with Russia (perhaps not de jure but de facto) did not produce much parliamentary activity. Similarly, by the time this book was submitted for publication, the House of Commons had voted twice on the missions aimed against the Islamic State; they produced some debates but were most useful for giving Stephen Harper the opportunity to manipulate the Liberals. The government indicated that the costs of the war would be classified, so it would not release the figures to Parliament.

Political parties certainly matter when extension votes are held, but parliamentary committees? Not so much. Will Parliament be reformed any time soon?[32] This is unlikely, so the best that Canadians can hope for is that the prime minister, the minister of national defence, and the CDS perform well on their own as the pressures emanating from Parliament are weak at best and ill-informed almost all of the time.

chapter six

Whole of Government
or Holes in Government?

The central irony of the Whole of Government (WG) idea is that governments are supposed to act coherently but that it takes tremendous effort to compel individual agencies to act jointly for even a short period of time, particularly in high-priority cases. Canada was widely admired for its WG effort in Afghanistan despite being a topic of much finger-pointing and criticism at home.[1] So many agencies were involved in the Canadian mission, many with a history of being poor partners, that any degree of cooperation whatsoever could be seen as a major victory. Any assessment of how Canada performed in Afghanistan has to take seriously the half-full/half-empty nature of the enterprise – that these agencies worked together more closely than ever before, doing things that many of them had never been trained or equipped to do, in an incredibly difficult context. The WG effort required a high level of attention, which was neither sustainable nor sustained, and the agencies involved learned a great deal from it. What remains to be seen is whether these lessons will be remembered the next time Canada needs a WG effort in a dangerous setting.

Three key events significantly shaped cooperation among the various agencies involved: the death of Glyn Berry in early 2006, the detainee controversy in 2007, and the Manley Report in 2008. The first essentially delayed the development of WG for a year; the second produced enough pressure to create some temporary cooperation; and the third provided a short burst of momentum that produced significant cooperation for a year and a set of structures that shaped the rest of the mission. Before going through each of these phases, the complexity of the WG effort needs to be unravelled by considering the panoply of agencies, interests, and cultures that shaped different outlooks on the mission.

The Agencies

The three most important Canadian agencies in Afghanistan were clearly DFAIT, CIDA, and the CF. But many other actors were involved, including the Department of Public Safety, the RCMP, and members of provincial police forces; CSC; the Canada Border Services Agency (CBSA); and the Canadian Security Intelligence Service (CSIS).

The CF was always the single largest and most influential Canadian actor in Kandahar. At its peak, it had nearly 3,000 troops in Afghanistan and nearby, supporting it in the region. It provided much of the staff to the PRT, all of the personnel for the battle group as well as logistical and command support at the KAF. The Canadian commander of the task force was one of the most important actors in Kandahar from 2006 to 2011. He had significant funds to spend on local development projects, interacted with Afghan officials at all levels, and could deploy various assets, including engineers, to address some of the development challenges.

Four key attitudes shaped how the CF worked with the civilians in theatre. First, there was a basic tendency in the army to see everyone else as "enablers," whose primary objective was to support the army.[2] Some junior officers in Kandahar went so far as to refer to the Canadian civilians in theatre as "disablers."[3] David Mulroney, the deputy minister who headed the task force in 2008–9, reported that this attitude was common not just among the junior officers – that to do COIN, the military needed civilians to help. His view was the reverse – that the military was there to enable the civilians to develop a more stable Afghanistan.[4]

The second attitude that shaped the relationship between the CF and the civilians on the ground came from the counter-insurgency manual that American General David Petraeus had developed in the mid-2000s. A key line in this manual asserts that there are certain tasks that civilians should be responsible for but are often not able to perform;[5] in this case, the military tends to assume these responsibilities. This attitude led many of the militaries in Afghanistan, including the CF, to become involved in development and governance projects with and without the cooperation of civilian agencies.

A third dynamic influencing civilian-military relations was the fact that each commander served for nine months or so, putting the focus very much on the short term. While Canada's operational command headquarters back home, Canadian Expeditionary Forces Command (CEFCOM), developed longer-term campaign plans, the regular rotation of commanders in the field, each with his distinct personality and priorities, meant that civilians had to adjust to each.

Last, the CF was part of a larger NATO-led effort, so it tended to look to ISAF for guidance and coordination rather than Ottawa. This meant that the CF was often a stubborn partner in the WG effort. The next chapter will address the role of the CF more fully, but here I concentrate on the CF as a partner in the WG effort.

DFAIT went from having a very small footprint in Afghanistan to a leading role, both in Kandahar and back home in Ottawa. Initially, Canada had a small embassy consisting of an ambassador (Chris Alexander), a political officer, a CIDA representative, and not much more.[6] Over time, however, it grew to be one of the larger Canadian embassies in the world. In Kandahar, DFAIT went from having one representative in 2006–7 to dozens within the span of a few years.[7] In the aftermath of the Manley Report, the position of RoCK was created, giving one person leadership of the entire civilian effort, with the intent to create a coequal to the commander of the task force. This position was staffed by a series of DFAIT officials. At the same time, a position was created in Ottawa to coordinate the entire Afghanistan effort: deputy minister of the Afghanistan Task Force in the Privy Council Office. The first person to hold this office was David Mulroney, a long-time DFAIT official who served for a year and was succeeded by Greta Bossenmaier. While the CF received most of the attention – and deservedly so – for the sacrifices it made, DFAIT gained pivotal positions, shaping what Canadians would be doing in Kandahar.

DFAIT had little frame of reference for this kind of effort. Other countries' foreign affairs departments had some expeditionary histories to fall back on, but Canada's had no such experience. Its officers were not trained to work in combat zones or to serve as trainers in governance, nor were they prepared in terms of insurance policies. Unlike the military, DFAIT officials were not insured if harmed in combat.[8] In the field, they were completely dependent on the CF for protection, which meant that their plans were often secondary to the CF's priorities of the day. Back home, DFAIT was initially quite fragmented in its approach, with multiple offices shouldering Afghan-related responsibilities. Before becoming the deputy minister to improve WG, Mulroney was tasked with creating a "whole of DFAIT" effort.[9]

Although DFAIT officers gained much valuable experience and the department as a whole played a central role in the Afghanistan mission, it was eclipsed in terms of public perception by the CF. Moreover, DFAIT officials in Ottawa and in the field had to constantly struggle to convince agencies to coordinate. Neither the CF nor CIDA was used to DFAIT running the show; both resisted frequently and often rather effectively. Nevertheless, the institutional innovations – the RoCK, a task force within DFAIT, and then the Afghan task force encompassing the entire whole of government effort – showed that DFAIT could learn and adapt to a difficult situation. While the various reports almost certainly overestimated the progress made in Kandahar, there is little doubt that DFAIT and its personnel evolved into one of the most admired WG efforts in Afghanistan.

CIDA received much criticism during the Afghanistan mission. Most of its efforts are aimed at national capitals, often carried out by international organizations and NGOs, and focused on long-term outcomes.[10] It therefore had relatively little experience running projects in conflict zones, especially those that were supposed to have a quick impact. CIDA personnel did not want Afghanistan to be a focus of their efforts given that its priority was poverty relief and not supporting Canadian diplomatic efforts.[11] The first CIDA representative on the PRT had little significant experience.[12]

My own encounter with CIDA's adviser to the Canadian task force commander, Brigadier-General Guy Laroche, in late 2007 was quite disappointing. I asked a basic question: If there is so much corruption in Afghanistan,[13] is there a way of determining the most egregious examples, combatting those, and tolerating the rest, which do not affect the larger effort as heavily? The CIDA person dismissed the idea, expressing the view that all forms of corruption were unacceptable. This might have been a good position from the standpoint of public relations, but it reflected an extreme naiveté about the problems facing the development effort.

CIDA faced a bigger problem – a very Ottawa-centric style of management. There was very little delegation to the CIDA representatives in the field,[14] which perhaps makes sense when development projects aim at decades-long processes. In a more fluid environment, however, where development projects are supposed to be coordinated with the rest of the effort, having to call back to Ottawa for most decisions made CIDA a tough agency with which to partner. Indeed, CF officers reported that they found the United States Agency for International Development (USAID) to be a much more helpful partner and only partly because it had bigger bags of cash. They preferred USAID because its officers on the ground had significant flexibility. Civilians, too, found CIDA a challenging partner. Participants in the WG mission noted that the effort to redirect CIDA required "significant negotiation" and that it delegated in name but was still centralized in spirit.[15] In interviews with former CIDA personnel, those who worked for NGOs, and others, a common complaint emerged – that CIDA officials rarely left the PRT.[16]

The fourth major government agency, the Department of Public Safety, was largely eclipsed by the first three, but it deployed a variety of actors to Kandahar, including the RCMP, CSC, CBSA, and CSIS. The effort to train the ANP was seen as a pivotal part of the COIN effort and of building rule of law in Kandahar. Canada sent not only Mounties but also officers from provincial police

forces (Ontario Provincial Police, Sûreté du Québec) and munici-
pal police from around Canada to participate in this training effort.
The kinds of police training varied with the particular individuals
serving in Kandahar as the RCMP took volunteers rather than trying to send officers with specific expertise. Thus, the training
courses would vary over time, depending on the number of officers and their skills. The basic approach was to give the officers a
fair amount of discretion, sending them out on patrol, often over-
night and at significant personal risk. Some officers were severely
wounded, but luckily, none were killed.[17]

While coordination with the CF was never a problem, the quali-
ty-quantity trade-off tended to be a point of contention. The CF
was focused on producing ever larger numbers of police, while the
RCMP was more focused on producing well-trained police. This
could be finessed by combining military and civilian police in
training courses to improve the Afghans' skill sets, but the different views about how to measure progress remained.[18]

CSC became heavily involved in mentoring staff at the Sarposa
prison to improve the conditions there. This was, of course, a key
effort because of its connection with the detainee controversy back
in Canada. The better treated the prisoners were in the Afghan
prisons, the better able the CF would be to transfer detainees. The
focus, then, was on training the warden and the prison guards as
well as seeking funds to improve the prison's infrastructure. Given
the state of the prison when Canadian personnel became involved,
it was a tall order. Public Safety personnel described the situation
as "practically insurmountable."[19]

The Waste of Whole of Government:
The Story of the Strategic Advisory Team in Kabul

Initial interactions between civilians and military officers in
Afghanistan were less than optimal. One of the military's most sig-
nificant initiatives, the Strategic Advisory Team of Afghanistan
(SAT-A), was opposed and then dismantled by the civilians. When

serving as commander of ISAF, Lt.-General Rick Hillier had positioned a team of Canadian colonels at the top of several Afghan government agencies to advise the Afghans, who were poorly equipped and lacked the training necessary to engage in governance.[20] This team left after Hillier's return to Canada but was essentially reinstated at President Hamid Karzai's request.[21] This initiative was supported at the time by Ambassador Chris Alexander and CIDA representative Nipa Banerjee. However, it met with strong resistance from the Canadian civilian agencies as it was seen as the military overreaching and working in areas best left to the civilians.[22] Indeed, Canada's next ambassador to Afghanistan, Arif Lalani, was particularly opposed to the SAT and eventually managed to kill it.[23] There was no civilian follow-up mission to supplant the program.[24]

This episode was quite revealing. It showed that the military was willing to go outside its lanes to solve a problem. It demonstrated that the civilian agencies were more than sceptical of such efforts, but neither willing nor able to replace the CF even in the relative safety of Kabul. It showed, in short, that before the Manley Panel had begun its work, WG was quite broken. At one time, Canadians were positioned in key nodes of the Afghan government and were providing skills that were highly desired by the president of Afghanistan. With this came significant influence, which, as a result of bureaucratic infighting, was ultimately wasted.

The Phases of Whole of Government in Kandahar

As we have seen, the Canadian WG effort made significant progress in Kandahar. It must be acknowledged, however, that this progress was neither inevitable nor steady. It is no accident that the most cohesive effort occurred in the aftermath of the Manley Panel or that this peak was relatively short-lived. Comparing the various phases of the effort, we can identify the trends that developed throughout the mission as well as the forces complicating Canada's role as a coherent player in Afghanistan.

In the initial stages, the non-military presence on the ground was quite thin and then became thinner still. The first key event was the death of Glyn Berry, the political director of the PRT, in a car bomb attack in January 2006. It had a "paralytic effect" for at least a few months,[25] sending shock waves through the Canadian political system. It largely froze the effort to build a civilian presence in Kandahar and essentially locked most of the civilians in the PRT behind the wire.[26] Throughout 2006–7, governance and development efforts took a back seat to combat operations in the province and beyond.

Strikingly, the first real attempt to develop a coordinated WG effort was a result of the detainee controversy. With the military under attack for its role in transferring detainees to the Afghans, the CF was more willing to cooperate, recognizing the need for civilian expertise to manage key aspects of a reformed process. To resolve the problem, Canada needed to monitor what happened to the detainees once they were turned over, to improve the training of the Afghans so that abuses would not happen (at least not as often), and to pressure the Afghan government to take the matter seriously. DFAIT deployed monitors to visit the prisons, CSC sent personnel to help train wardens and guards, the RCMP helped to train the ANP, and DFAIT coordinated the whole process. The new agreement with Afghanistan was signed after six weeks of WG effort.[27] However, not all agencies were so willing to help: CIDA stayed out of it entirely.[28]

The aftermath of the Manley Panel produced the peak in WG efforts and coordination thanks to key institutional innovation both in Ottawa and Kandahar.[29] In Ottawa, the Afghanistan Task Force was situated within the Privy Council Office, acting on behalf of the Cabinet Committee on Afghanistan and headed by a deputy minister, David Mulroney, with access to the Clerk of the Privy Council and with the support of the prime minister. Mulroney was not only very experienced on the Afghanistan file from his previous postings in DFAIT but was considered to be a very tough bureaucratic combatant – someone who would "bring a gun to a knife fight."[30] Consequently, the various agencies had to deal with an empowered official who not only had significant heft because of his position within the Privy Council Office and the Manley and parliamentary mandates but also possessed a willingness to "break eggs."[31]

At the same time, the RoCK position was established in Kandahar, empowering a single DFAIT official to shepherd all of the Canadian civilian efforts in the province. The first RoCK was Elissa Golberg, who had served as executive director on the Manley Panel. She had significant cachet as a result of her experience and reputation as well as a strong connection to Mulroney. Various departments, particularly CIDA, did not want to invest the RoCK with significant authority, but after immense pressure from the Cabinet and Prime Minister's Office, it was given some tools to facilitate coordination on the ground.[32]

The key tools that both Mulroney and Golberg had to promote coordination were the newly enunciated six priorities and three signature projects.[33] The six priorities were:

- Maintain a more secure environment and establish law and order by building the capacity of the ANA and ANP.
- Provide jobs, education, and essential services.
- Provide humanitarian assistance to people in need.
- Enhance the management and security of the Afghanistan-Pakistan border.
- Build Afghan institutions and support democratic processes such as elections.
- Contribute to Afghan-led political reconciliation efforts. [34]

The three signature projects were the rehabilitation of the Dahla Dam, the construction of at least 50 schools, and the eradication of polio. These priorities and projects provided a focus for the civilian effort as Canadian governance and development workers could not do everything – Kandahar had a great many needs. Combined with quarterly reports, the priorities were a way for Mulroney to press the agencies involved to meet the various targets. The signature projects were aimed at producing visible progress, which could be sold back home as Canada's contribution to Kandahar and to Afghanistan.

There has been and will continue to be much discussion and debate about why these particular efforts were chosen. For instance, the Dahla Dam presented a tremendous set of challenges since most of the work would take place far outside the security bubbles that the CF had established. That particular choice has been called foolish by development experts as much of the money dedicated to the project had to be spent on private security companies.[35] Indeed, the choice of the dam reflected a conflict between the military, which preferred to focus on providing more electricity to Kandahar, and the civilians, who thought irrigation was a more pressing need.[36] There was a bigger conflict between the military and civilians about the centrality of the six priorities and three projects, and I will address this below. The key point here is that the mission gained a greater focus for a time.

However, the focus that coordinated the WG effort started to fade. The agencies resisted the coordination efforts mightily. An example of this was the military's routine of sending colonels and lieutenant-colonels to key meetings, knowing that they could not formally make decisions but would have to refer things to their superior officers. CIDA was reluctant to share information "to the point of dishonesty."[37] After six months, Mulroney realized that he was running out of momentum, and by the end of his year in the post, it was clear that those above him (including Stephen Harper) had lost interest in the mission. As Mulroney expressed after the fact, he had felt that he was becoming part of the problem.[38] His successor, Greta Bossenmaier, was not as aggressive in the post and did not have some of the advantages Mulroney had had.[39] Work would continue on the six priorities and the three signature projects, but the WG effort would face more stress at the seams.

Priorities, Outputs, and Outcomes

The aforementioned priorities were designed by Canadian officials to provide visible and measurable progress, mostly in Kandahar, to demonstrate that Canada was making a difference and to show that its investment in blood and treasure was paying off. Viewed another, perhaps more cynical, way, the priorities were Canada's *exit strategy*, giving officials something to point to when the CF left the province and as the civilians started to go home.

The final report on Canada's engagement in Afghanistan includes many indicators to show that Canadians made a significant effort.

- 33 of 44 targets achieved.
- Rule of law benchmarks and targets met or surpassed for policing, corrections, and justice.
- 52 schools, two more than targeted; training of 3,000 teachers; literacy training to 27,000 Kandaharis; vocational training to 6,500.
- Rehabilitation of the Dahla Dam;[40] significant increases in irrigated land.
- Health care improved, with 2,000 health care workers trained.
- Support of the Dubai process: improving relations between Afghanistan and Pakistan.
- Better border policing through training of the Afghan Border Police.
- Electoral reform.
- Human rights improvement through support of the Afghanistan Independent Human Rights Commission.
- 386,690 children vaccinated in the anti-polio effort.[41]

Despite these impressive figures, one part of the report is particularly telling: it describes the dangers of relying on this kind of metric in assessing the overall Canadian effort in Afghanistan.

All Canadian infrastructure, equipment and training efforts with respect to corrections were *completed and all targets were met*.... All of this training and mentoring contributed to a *better equipped and a better run prison* compared to that of 2008. However, despite considerable efforts by Canada, the international community and the Afghan Central Prisons Directorate and other Afghan leaders, *challenges persist* in creating a more modern correctional system in Afghanistan. This reality was *underscored by the mass escape* of more than 480 inmates from Sarpoza Prison earlier in 2011.[42]

Canada focused much of its effort on improving the prisons in Kandahar. This made sense not only as a way to respond to the detainee controversy and to be in compliance with international law but also from a COIN perspective. Prisons are prime recruiting grounds for insurgencies; if Canada and Afghanistan could improve conditions, it would reduce a major source of Taliban recruits.

Yet one of the most basic but perhaps under-appreciated features of a successful prison is the ability to keep the prisoners inside. Many will remember the coordinated Taliban attack on the Sarposa prison in 2008, which led to the escape of hundreds of inmates.[43] In 2011, shortly before the Canadians pulled out, another escape at the same prison occurred as outsiders dug a tunnel into it. This represented a massive failure on three counts: it was clear that the outsiders had inside help, the prison was not prepared for the possibility of tunnelling,[44] and the CF and its allies had poor intelligence about the neighbourhood around the prison.

It may seem unfair to use the example of prisons to represent the relative successes and failures of the WG effort. It is true that the prisons were in abysmal shape before the Canadians became serious about improving them, so one could talk of improvement from a very low baseline yet still fall short of a successful prison (one that keeps the prisoners inside). But the prison was perhaps one of the efforts that most unified the Canadian team. And it did so because it was one of the projects that most closely tied together Canadian interests (dealing with the detainee challenge) and NATO's (doing COIN better).

Indeed, one of the biggest problems with most of the Canadian projects cited above is that they were *outputs*, not *outcomes*. And the outcomes were not tied so clearly to the larger NATO effort. What do 50 or 52 schools have to do with anything? Yes, Canada left more schools behind when it left the province than when it started, but were there classes being held in all of those schools in July

2011?[45] More important, what was the impact of those schools on the legitimacy of the Afghan government? On the support of the Kandaharis for the ISAF effort to fight the Taliban? The signature projects had a very basic flaw: the temptation to hoist a Canadian flag over them meant that the Afghan people did not see their own government as providing these improvements – the irrigation, the schools, the eradication of polio.[46] Since the goal of the effort was to build a self-sustaining Afghan government, it is not clear how the signature projects helped the Afghans. What was important to the Canadians was that putting the Canadian flag on these projects meant that they could be sold back home. In Afghanistan, there was often the admonition to make sure that an effort had an "Afghan face" on it, but the people of Kandahar could almost certainly figure out who was doing the work. In terms of making progress there, the questions that needed to be asked again and again were: How does this affect the war? How does it encourage Afghans to side with the government and ISAF?

Some of the priorities were directly connected to the larger war: improving the rule of law and training the ANA and ANP, improving border police and customs, providing vocational training for young men who might otherwise become insurgents, and so on. As far as other priorities were concerned, the connection was more tenuous. The WG effort had a built-in fissure – between the civilians, focused on the demands of Ottawa, and the military, focused in large part on fighting the war. The civilian effort was focused on meeting the objectives set by Ottawa, viewing the military as enablers who would help tick off the various checklists related to the quarterly reports. The military effort, on the other hand, was focused on defeating the Taliban, viewing the civilians as enablers who would provide the governance and development efforts that might not win hearts and minds but could perhaps build some confidence among the Afghans in ISAF and, more important, in the Afghan government. One indicator of this divide is that CF officers kept finding their discussion of COIN progress being scrubbed out of the quarterly reports.[47]

In conversations with Canadian civilians, it is clear that their priority was fulfilling the promises built into the parliamentary vote and the Afghanistan Task Force's list of priorities and projects. This list did provide focus and consistency from 2008 to 2011, which the mission badly needed. The CF's efforts tended to shift focus with each new commander, a transition that took place every nine months or so. On the other hand, the commanders on the ground were adapting to changes in the war – the ebbs and flows of Taliban efforts, the increased centralization of the war at ISAF headquarters, changes in the number of troops in Kandahar, lessons learned about what was working better, etc. There should have been a better balance between consistency and adaptation. However, because the civilians and the military had very different views of what was at stake – proving that Canada had an impact versus fighting the war – and because they had different management styles – centralization versus delegation – the Canadian effort had a hard time bridging these differences.

Whole of Government Lessons and Conclusions[48]

While the WG effort in Ottawa was perhaps not as deep or wide as advertised, it was a far more coordinated effort than would have been possible without the Manley Panel and without the institutional reforms that took place, and it was seen as being far more successful than the efforts made by other countries.[49] We are not likely to see an effort like this again given that the unique circumstances surrounding the Afghanistan mission are not likely to be replicated – the direct attention of a prime minister, the creation of a deputy ministerial position for a particular intervention, the appointment of an official with a willingness to fight very tenaciously (Mulroney), and the other events we have reviewed in this chapter.

Instead, we see old patterns emerging. Despite the presence of 900 soldiers and the investment of millions of dollars, the Afghanistan Task Force was quickly disbanded. There is now one civilian working the Afghan file at DND; there are a few working on Afghanistan at DFAIT, a much smaller team than a few years ago.[50] To undertake an effective intervention, civilians and military must train together ahead of time, but civilians lack the military's capacity to deploy to a training site and work things out for a few weeks; they must continue to work their "day jobs" until they deploy, with little time for exercises.

Like most modern militaries, the CF engages in serious after-action, lessons-learned exercises after operations; this enables it to develop ideas about which adaptations and innovations were successful and less successful and to disseminate them to the next generations of officers. For the first time,[51] it seems that civilians were also seeking to identify the lessons learned from the Afghanistan experience. This would be an encouraging development, but it is one that is entirely undercut by the fact that a document produced by the Privy Council Office describing these lessons learned is currently buried.[52]

Despite years of coordinated efforts in Kandahar and Ottawa, key institutional obstacles remain.[53] For one, there are no rewards in any Canadian agency for individuals who play well with those in other agencies. Promotions remain the reward for serving the particular agency rather than the broader, shared effort. Perhaps the Canadian government can learn lessons from how the CF unified in the late 1960s, so that its members would identify with and act on behalf of the CF rather than the army or navy or air force. The US military does a far better job than it once did in that its Joint Staff thinks *jointly* rather than about the air force, army, etc.[54] Achieving this required institutional innovation; giving officers incentives to work in joint billets, including making such work a requirement for promotion. Thus far, we have seen little such interest in the Canadian government to improve WG for the long run, although the merger of CIDA with DFAIT might mean better coordination between governance and development efforts in the future.

There are organizational cultural dynamics that are simply hard to overcome. For instance, DFAIT and CIDA officials change positions in the summer so that their children can change schools with little disruption.[55] This can produce a loss of institutional memory during the most active part of the year.

In discussing organizations, it is important to keep in mind how crucial personalities are. Some military officers were better equipped to work with DFAIT, such as Brigadier-General Denis Thompson. Many interviewees cited his partnership with Elissa Golberg as the best working tandem among the combinations of RoCK and task force commander,[56] perhaps because he is married to a DFAIT official. Since we are unlikely to require Canadian commanders to marry government officials for the sake of future WG efforts, it is hard to see how replicable this moment in Afghanistan can be. It is also the case that cross-agency cooperation tended to function better on the ground than it did back home. The soldiers and civilians on the ground faced far more pressure to get along than the agencies who were removed from the actual, day-to-day realities of the effort. In addition, being co-located at the KAF or at the PRT helped develop relationships and trust, something that simply never prospers much among agencies distributed around Ottawa.

Looking at Canada's efforts towards Afghanistan, more effort was made to improve the WG approach than perhaps any other aspect of Canada's involvement there. The adaptations were significant, the authorities were concentrated, and there was even some delegation to the field in the form of the RoCK. The good news is that the Canadian civilian agencies adapted quite significantly in the face of this very serious test. The WG effort was not perfect, as we have seen. The biggest flaw is that it failed to bridge the divide between the civilian agencies and the military as far as what Canada was attempting to do – complete a checklist in Kandahar or help to gain momentum in a COIN effort. Despite the many gains made, this essential divide suggests that the whole of Canadian government still has room to improve. To be fair, however, this problem bedevilled most of the countries operating in Afghanistan.

chapter seven

The Canadian Forces: Winners?

One of the most striking contrasts one will find when considering the Canadian experience in and since Afghanistan involves the Canadian Forces. In the collective mind of the senior officers, the Afghanistan effort was a major success. The best evidence of this might be that nearly every Canadian who commanded in Afghanistan has been promoted.[1] However, if you ask the public, experts on Afghanistan, or officials in other Canadian agencies, Kandahar does not seem to be such a success story.[2] This presents the potential for a credibility gap as the very positive perspective presented by the CF may cause others to discount whatever senior officers may say in the future.

To be clear, the CF did quite well, but where? In this chapter, I first consider three arenas in which it gained significant success: within the military, within NATO, and within Canada. The war helped to cement a cultural revolution within the CF that mitigated the risk aversion imposed by the Somalia experience. In terms of its membership in NATO, the CF, in the words of General Rick Hillier, went from being "Can'tbats" to being among the most reliable forces in the alliance. In Canada, the war changed how the CF was perceived, enabling it to shed the blue helmet mythology. Notice that none of these arenas are Kandahar, which I go on to address. Next, I consider the impact that the Afghanistan experience has and will have on the CF.

Changing How the Canadian Forces Fight[3]

The cloud of Somalia had hung over the CF for about a decade.[4] There were many lessons learned and perhaps over-learned, including avoidance of risk and the use of restrictive rules of engagement. Hillier recounts how the British took the NATO jargon for *Canadian battalions*, "Canbats" (like "UKbats," "USbats," and so on), and called the CF deployed with them in Bosnia "Can'tbats."[5] This referred to the Canadians often saying that they could not do x or y when called upon by NATO commanders. An entire generation of officers chafed under the restrictions imposed by their senior officers.

When the Canadian forces were sent to Kandahar in early 2002 as their contribution to OEF, they faced the same rules that a fighter pilot would face – that any moves that might increase the risk of casualties or collateral damage had to receive permission from generals back in Ottawa. The commander of this deployment, Lt.-Colonel Pat Stogran, was seriously concerned about how limited his discretion was, that his troops might have to be witnesses to war crimes rather than stopping them.[6] The effect of these restrictions was to limit much of the Canadian deployment in Kandahar to guarding the KAF, although Canadians did contribute to some notable efforts, including Operation Anaconda.[7]

While there was some learning back in Ottawa between this mission and the next in Kabul, the troops sent to the ISAF effort that was focused entirely on Kabul still had very limited discretion. Canadian General Peter Devlin, serving as commander of NATO's forces in Kabul in 2003–4, viewed the Canadian contingent as being in the middle tier of reliability as the CF faced fairly restrictive rules about how to do its business.[8] His successor, Brigadier-General Jocelyn Lacroix, also received restrictive orders. "*NDHQ [National Defence Headquarters] authority is required*, prior to committing CF [Canadian Forces] personnel to *any operations*, wherein there is a reasonable belief that CF units or personnel may be *exposed to a higher degree of risk*."[9] These telephone calls home often took a day or more, which meant that the NATO commanders on the ground had to look elsewhere for troops willing to respond to events as they occurred.[10]

The highlight of Canada's early involvement in Afghanistan occurred when Lieutenant-General Rick Hillier became commander of the entire ISAF mission. However, this was a very frustrating experience for him as he did not have actual command of the Canadian contingent serving in Afghanistan. A Canadian colonel served in that role, with the result that Hillier would have to ask the colonel for permission to use the CF in Afghanistan, and that colonel often had to say no.[11]

This pattern of limited discretion and frustration ended in 2005–6. When the Canadians deployed to southern Afghanistan, the commanders arrived with new rules that allowed them to make decisions as situations arose. They could and did not only plan operations in their sector – the province of Kandahar – but also respond to events in neighbouring ones to help out the British in Helmand, the Dutch in Uruzgan, and the Americans in Zabul. Colonel Steve Noonan reported that he had "wide arcs of fire,"[12] with orders that were significantly broader than those of his predecessors.[13] Brigadier-General David Fraser, who commanded during Operation Medusa, Canada's bloodiest battle since Korea,[14] reported, "Everything I did over there was notification, not approval…. If I had to go outside the boundaries of the CDS intent, then I would have to get approval. I never got to a boundary."[15] The official Letter of Intent that the CDS gave to Fraser contrasts sharply with those given to earlier commanders.

> Within the bounds of the Strategic Targeting Directive, you have *full freedom to authorize and conduct operations as you see fit.* In the interest of national situational awareness, *whenever possible* you are to inform me [CEFCOM] in advance of the concept of operations for any planned operations, particularly those likely to involve significant contact with the enemy.[16]

This pattern held up through to the end of the Kandahar mission. Commanders from Noonan onward reported operating in a completely different command environment than they had in previous missions in Bosnia and elsewhere.[17] This was the product of a generational change within the CF – senior officers who had reacted to the Somalia affair by becoming risk averse and leery were delegating to younger officers who chafed under these restrictions. Hillier, who reports his frustrations in his memoir,[18] was not alone. Most of the officers I interviewed had served in Bosnia or earlier in Afghanistan and found it embarrassing and frustrating to say no to their NATO partners, that Canada could not help out when called upon. As a result, when they were put in a position to change how Canada operated, they did.

Hillier set up CEFCOM to run overseas deployments.[19] This new command was located in a building on the outskirts of Ottawa to distance the operational command from the rest of the DND hierarchy. The job of CEFCOM commander rotated among the Canadian Army's Afghan hands, from Lt.-General Mike Gauthier to Lt.-General Marc Lessard to Lt.-General Stuart Beare. With a greater understanding of the "ground truth," they were willing to delegate to the commanders on the ground, although they varied in how much oversight they conducted – Gauthier visited Kandahar and queried commanders far more often than his successors.

The reorganization and the new orders going into the field were almost entirely an intra-CF process. The minister of national defence at the time of these reforms was Bill Graham, who later indicated, "I counted on the military to decide how best to organize itself, and Hillier came up with restructuring to handle interventions abroad."[20] The same largely applied to changes in Canadian caveats. The Germans responded to Canadian complaints about the restrictions on the German forces, which prevented them from helping in Kandahar, by saying that the Canadians also had caveats. Hillier's response was to look for any restrictions on Canadian troops, such as not engaging in crowd control, and eliminate them after chatting with the minister.[21]

Hillier insisted that his reforms to the structures and pattern of delegation were the only way to go – empowering the commanders on the ground and supporting them with whatever they needed. In my interview with him, it was striking that there seemed to be no other way to do it. He argued that spending so much time and money training officers meant that it made little sense to make decisions in Ottawa when the personnel in place in the field could better assess the situations and decide. This contrasted sharply with the views of Vice-Admiral (ret.) Gregg Maddison, who was deputy chief of the defence staff before Hillier was CDS: he displayed far more caution and referred to Somalia without being prompted,[22] unlike any of the officers of the new generation.

From "Can't bat" to "Can Do"

The change in how the Canadians fought altered how they were perceived by their allies. Canada went from being among the unreliable forces to being one of the few reliable. Canadian commanders no longer had to be embarrassed when asked to participate in a NATO operation; instead, they could participate and even lead. Command of RC-S rotated among the British, the Dutch, and the Canadians. While this decision preceded Canada's deployment, Canadian leadership would have been greatly undercut had the CF been restricted, as in the recent past. In response to a question about caveats, a senior NATO officer commented that things in Afghanistan would be going well if he just had more Americans, British, Australians, and Canadians and the helicopters needed to move them around the country.[23]

The willingness to move its small force out of Kandahar to help out its allies as they settled into the neighbouring provinces probably did more to change the CF's "street cred" than anything else. Also, Operation Medusa demonstrated what the CF was willing to do and what some of Canada's allies were not willing to do.[24] Thus, the increase in Canada's status within NATO is relative to the decline of the reputation of Germany and other more restricted countries.

In NATO, decision-making used to be apportioned strictly by the size of the contingent that each country provided to a mission. In my year working on the US Joint Staff, I helped to organize a meeting of the major players in NATO's Balkan missions. It was called the Quint as it included five countries – the United States, the United Kingdom, France, Germany, and Italy – the countries providing the largest contingents to the Balkan efforts. When I organized the dinner for that meeting, there was not even a "kids' table" for the rest of NATO. As things developed in Afghanistan, influence in the mission depended on not just the size of the force but also what a contingent was willing to do. Germany and Italy were essentially moved to the kids' table of ISAF decision-making, and Canadian officers were placed at the main table. Sure, most decisions were still made by American generals paying attention to American politicians back home, but Canadian officers had more opportunities to influence what ISAF was doing. Canadian officers served in many prominent positions in the ISAF chain of command rather than being strategy consumers, as had been the case in prior NATO efforts.[25]

When the United States reinforced the Canadians in Kandahar in the aftermath of the Manley Report, it served under Canadian command. This represented a significant measure of trust for American forces, who are rarely willing to subordinate themselves to commanders from other countries. During my interviews with Canadian, American, and other officers, one word – trust – was mentioned far more often than I ever could have anticipated.[26]

Why would Canadian officers want to change their standing in NATO? First, more influence is more influence.[27] Canadian officers clearly believed that they would be better used on the battlefield if they had some say about it. They knew their contingent's capabilities best, they were trained to think that they were good at what they did, and they trusted themselves and those with whom they had trained more than semi-random NATO officers assigned to be above them in their chain of command. Second, there were obvious self-esteem issues involved – if your organization was more respected, you would feel better about yourself and your organization. It was far easier to maintain morale if the units of other countries respected your troops and your leadership. Third, officers are ambitious, or else they would not rise very far in the military. So they wanted more responsibility and more credit when opportunities presented themselves. Having a better reputation within

NATO would give officers better chances to lead, succeed, and move up. And they were right: nearly every Canadian commander who served in Afghanistan returned home to be promoted to higher and more influential positions.

The War Back Home

A journalist asked me in the early days of the effort, can the CF fight? Are its soldiers trained to engage in combat? This was a result of the "decade of darkness," as Hillier and others call it,[28] when the military faced budget cuts, and of the peacekeeping that Canada had been doing.[29] I had to inform the journalist that the military saw combat as its primary job – its day job, if you will – and that it could, in fact, do combat.[30] After six years in Kandahar, no one was asking whether the CF could fight. This was clearly something that the current generation of CF officers wanted – to be seen as warriors and not as peacekeepers.

The most obvious evidence of this is the title of Rick Hillier's memoir: *A Soldier First*. The book concludes as follows:

> Everyone who wore a uniform had experienced a cultural revolution. We were proud to wear our uniforms, but we also had confidence in who we were – warriors first and foremost, able to do any task – with a first responsibility to finish tough, often violent tasks when Canada needed them done.... The immense frustration at the ignorance of so many who labeled us "only" peacekeepers had disappeared.[31]

Hillier is far blunter than most officers, but he is not alone in emphasizing war-fighting. I have attended several conferences and workshops held by the CF since Hillier's retirement, and a senior officer always makes a speech invoking the warrior or the war-fighter as the CF's key role.[32]

The decade of darkness after Somalia was not just about the shame and the budget cuts but also about the frustration at being viewed as just blue-helmeted peacekeepers. This was especially galling since Canadian soldiers fought and were hurt during some of these UN peacekeeping operations. There was also much frustration with the dominance of "soft power" as the defining narrative of Canadian foreign policy as this deliberately sidelined those involved in the harder forms of power – the CF.

I do not mean to argue that Hillier advocated going into Kandahar in 2005 to change the reputation of the CF in Canada, although some do.[33] Instead, the Kandahar mission meshed well with a larger imperative for Hillier and his generation of officers – to make a visible difference and to lead. That decision had a variety of consequences, including changing how Canadians see the CF. Thus, they can look back and see the mission as a success, even as that raises more than a few problems.

Kandahar as a Success Story?

It is so very hard to assess progress in a COIN effort. In a conventional war, you measure winning and losing by the amount of territory gained or lost and the number of casualties taken on both sides. In an unconventional war, winning means having the people support the government more than the insurgents, but public displays of support are quite risky indeed. A key problem in all of this is that the relationship between insurgent activities and counterinsurgent efforts is complex. There may have been little active insurgency before the Canadians moved into Kandahar in 2005, but as the number of foreign troops increased, it provided the insurgents with more targets and more opportunities. In the COIN efforts in Iraq and Afghanistan, we saw more significant enemy activity as the Americans surged, but it would be somewhat deceptive to suggest that outsiders caused the insurgency. No, they increased insurgent activity aimed against them, but the insurgents would have been fine to have territories and populaces to themselves, uncontested. Consequently, to determine whether a mission is having success, observers have to rely on proxies as polling in a war zone can be less than reliable. I heard one senior NATO officer say that he had more than 60 different metrics (measures) of success, which means that he did not really have a single good one.[34]

Conflicting reports emanated from Kandahar. For much of the mission, the CF had entirely too small a force to control any spot of territory. Its battle group would go out to disrupt the Taliban, but that was only the first part of the COIN mantra of "clear, hold, build." The CF really held only Kandahar City for much of its time in the province. Operation Medusa in 2006, which was one of the CF's costliest engagements, did not establish control or enduring support in Panjway, but it did help to prevent the loss of Kandahar City itself. Some have speculated that the Taliban's aim was to produce a Tet Offensive–like outcome: if they could successfully penetrate Kandahar, it might turn public opinion in Canada against the war.[35] The CF prevented the Taliban from earning such a victory.

Once the Americans surged into Kandahar, there were enough forces to concentrate and do some building. The new village protection plan in the Dand District seemed to be working in 2010–11, but conditions were especially ripe for winning over the local population since the residents belonged to tribes that were enemies of those populating the Taliban.[36]

The phrase "hearts and minds" is well known, but the real question was one of confidence. Could those Afghans sympathetic to the government and to the external interveners be sure that they would be protected? Could they risk their lives by giving intelligence tips to the government and to ISAF? Could they participate in the development projects without fear of retribution? While one could see signs of progress over the course of the Canadian effort, in terms of roads paved and schools built, it was not clear that the Canadians and their allies were able to gain much Afghan confidence. After all, there were two massive prison breaks in a three-year span. One could blame the Afghans running the prison, but it happened in Kandahar City, suggesting that the CF did not have good situational awareness. Perceptions are key in these kinds of conflicts, and it would have been strange for the Afghans to have much confidence, especially after the second prison break in 2011. Moreover, more than a few of the Afghans with whom Canada worked closely were assassinated in 2010–11, again shaking the confidence of the people who might be willing to work with the Canadians.

There is no doubt that the CF made a difference, holding onto Kandahar and keeping the Taliban mostly at bay despite being dramatically understaffed. Many of the allies did not show up when called on for help. The Americans, the British, and the Danes were most reliable; the Australians and the Dutch helped out; but the rest of NATO and its partners tended to disappoint the CF.[37] The CF did adapt to its circumstances, and it sacrificed a lot. That progress was elusive had much to do with the Afghan partners, Pakistan's support of the Taliban across the border, and the complexities of working in a corrupted narco-state. Still, given the wreckage that is the Afghan government, attempts to declare success will cause observers to question the CF's credibility. Of course, the true measure of the NATO effort in Afghanistan will be taken in the future: will the Afghan government manage to stay in place after the outsiders go home?

The Enduring Impact of Afghanistan on the Canadian Forces

There may be such a thing as too much avowed success. Being the most visible and most flexible Canadian entity for much of a decade may be causing a backlash against the CF.[38] While it improved its reputation at home and abroad, it has raised concerns, legitimate or not, that will shape how it is deployed and how it is perceived in the near future. Because the CF proved to be adaptive to the dynamics on the ground and became less risk averse, Stephen Harper and perhaps other politicians may have learned that putting it into harm's way reduces their control over events. This may lead to more carefully designed interventions or none at all. A second impact of the mission, due to its poor timing during the 2008 financial crisis, may be on the force structure and operations of the military down the road. A third set of concerns focuses on fears of the militarization of Canadian foreign policy. I address these dynamics briefly here before returning to the potential credibility problem.

Learning Not to Deploy

As discussed earlier in this book and elsewhere,[39] Stephen Harper apparently likes to have tight control over what Canadian officials do and say. Message management has been a cornerstone of his administration, whether it is a minority or majority government. The Canadian military is a particularly difficult agency for any politician. The CF's actions, whether mistaken or intended, can make the news faster and more visibly than any other part of the government. Canadian institutions provide much confusion about who is commander in chief, although that role is played by the governor general. The *perceived* tradition is that civilians tell the military where to deploy, and the military decides how it is done. The reality is more complex than that, but efforts by civilians to micromanage a mission move responsibility for casualties and any errors most clearly onto the civilians.

Message-managing the military is complicated by both history and reality. One of the consequences of the Somalia affair was legislation that allowed any CF member to talk to the media. This combines with the reality that a couple of thousand soldiers on the ground in the presence of embedded media means that there can be no message managing anyway. Thus, to send troops into harm's way means losing control of the messaging, something that the Harper government has been loath to do.

But the Conservatives can adapt as well, and this is reflected in the distinct pattern of recent Canadian missions. If you cannot control what the soldiers, sailors, and pilots of the CF can say, design the missions to limit what there is to say. The training mission in Afghanistan that began in 2011 as Canada withdrew from Kandahar was designed to minimize the risks of anything bad happening but also the risks that any divergent messages might come out of the country. The mission involved sending experienced officers and senior enlisted personnel to work on a variety of bases around Afghanistan (but not Kandahar). The training occurred only on bases – a big change from the previous efforts of embedding Canadian soldiers in Afghan units. The Canadians were not to leave these bases except to transfer to other bases or go out of the country. This not only limited their exposure to the insurgents but also limited how interesting they were to the media. The stories they could tell were simply not as colourful or newsworthy.

The next Canadian deployment was of a squadron of planes and one ship to the Libyan operation, which was not insignificant but far less risky and costly than a battle group to Afghanistan. "No boots on the ground" was the mantra for all NATO countries (except the United Kingdom and France, which deployed some SOF units). Canada embraced this, and as a result, the only CF personnel at risk were the few pilots dropping bombs on Libyan targets. The deployment also provided a smaller target for the media – reporters could talk only to the pilots and the personnel maintaining the planes. The Mali mission was even more restricted – to just one transport plane. It received some news coverage, but it did not last long as journalists found little interesting to report. The troops sent to Iraq in 2014 and beyond are SOF, so the media has very limited access to them and to the pilots flying the various missions in Iraqi and later Syrian airspace.[40]

A notable exception was a pivotal briefing in early 2015 that revealed that the Canadian SOF had been under fire and had been doing more than what the opposition had expected – in fact, the soldiers had been at the front lines about 20 per cent of the time.[41] Journalists suggested that this transparency was a mistake,[42] but, in retrospect, it seems like a clever move by the Harper government given that polls leaned towards support in the aftermath of the attack on Parliament in October 2014. It put the Liberals and Justin Trudeau in an awkward position as that party is stuck in the middle between aggressive Conservatives and pacifist New Democrats. Moreover, Trudeau has proved that he handles defence issues poorly. Given that the general who commanded the overall mission to Iraq in 2014, Lieutenant-General Jonathan Vance, commander of Canadian Joint Operations Command, was named CDS a few months later, it is hard to believe that the apparent openness in January was an accident or a mistake. Instead, the government can be transparent on military matters when it is politically advantageous and opaque when it is not.

Of course, another key Harper priority also accounts for this pattern and for the unlikeliness of another major ground deployment: balancing the budget. The financial crisis of 2008 led to spending less on the military. The focus of the cuts has been not on personnel, as that would violate a promise to keep the CF at 100,000 (regulars and reserves), but on operational readiness.[43]

The more enduring lesson of Afghanistan for Harper and his successors, given the CF's new attitude towards managing rather than avoiding risk, may simply be not to send significant numbers of troops into riskier enterprises. This solves the two-step problem of the risks of putting troops into combat and putting troops in a position where they might have interesting things to say to the media.

Computing the Costs

Any significant military deployment will be expensive. Afghanistan proved to be incredibly costly both in lives and in dollars, with estimates ranging from $14 billion to $22 billion.[44] Here I address the financial dimension. The mission began before the 2008 financial crisis, when the fiscal picture in Canada seemed to be unaffected by the cost of deploying a mission to Kandahar. Of course, this is only in comparison to the post-2008 climate since Hillier was at first given a strict budget envelope, which constrained his planning. Still, the key is how things looked after 2008. The need to buy or lease new equipment, the costs of deploying ever more soldiers, the escalation in aid budgets, and the medical costs of taking care of the wounded all put significant pressure on the Canadian budget. While there are many reasons why so many Canadian defence procurement programs have been delayed and stretched out, it is likely that the costs of combat in Kandahar crowded out other spending, or at least the attention needed to do that spending. As the government shifted its focus to deficit reduction, money spent on deployments became quite problematic. Indeed, this led to the strange business where the defence minister rather dramatically underestimated the expense of the Libya mission – although it was nevertheless pretty inexpensive compared to any major deployment.[45] Stranger still was the decision to consider the costs of the Iraq/Syria mission to be a Cabinet secret, preventing Parliament from knowing how expensive the mission would be, and then releasing the latest estimates to the media.[46]

The various goals in the Canada First Defence Strategy have not been met, nor will they be met at any time in the near future.[47] The army, which received the lion's share of the defence dollars during the deployment to Afghanistan, can only be at the back of the line as the navy and air force are finally able to pursue their modernization programs. Well, maybe, as even these efforts are going to face the budget axe to some degree. Already we have seen significant cuts to operations and maintenance, thereby raising concerns about the readiness of the CF. Given the increased reticence of the Conservatives to deploy the CF, as we saw above, this may not be so problematic in the short term. In the long term, however, the CF is likely to find itself underfunded, out of shape, ill prepared and under-equipped. Committing so heavily to Afghanistan might have been extremely positive for the military in some ways, but it is hard to see how it was good for the purchase of the next generation of weapons or for the maintenance of the CF's readiness.

The Militarization of Canada and Canadian Foreign Policy

For part of a decade, the Canadian Forces were the most visible and perhaps most influential Canadian organization in the making of foreign policy. The Stein and Lang book suggests that the CF essentially hoodwinked the civilians to put the troops into Kandahar.[48] This conventional wisdom, which I addressed in Chapter 3, shapes perceptions today, even if it is wrong. There is a concern that the CF has too much influence, that it stepped out of its lanes, and that Canada's position in the world is defined by its military.[49] Of course, this concern is somewhat overplayed.

The reality is that civilians still control the military and were responsible for all of the big decisions during the Afghanistan experience – where to deploy, when to withdraw, the basic objectives, and so on. Jean Chrétien and his Cabinet made the decision to go to Kandahar in the aftermath of 9/11 and later to go to Kabul. Paul Martin made the decision to send the CF to Kandahar, and if he has buyer's remorse, then so be it. Stephen Harper decided to extend the mission twice and then fully embraced the end of the Kandahar effort in 2011.[50] He decided, with little feedback from anyone, to send a training mission to Afghanistan in 2011 that ended in 2014.[51] And, of course, while the chain of command goes up from the CDS to the governor general, the governor general acts on the advice of the prime minister, who, in practice, picks the CDS and can ask him or her to step down. Thus, Canada's foreign policy is safely in the hands of civilians.

To be sure, a more assertive CF, in the guise of Rick Hillier but also the new set of commanders, means that the CF is a significant political player. This, combined with its higher profile during the Afghanistan mission, means that the military has more influence. Hillier was willing to speak out in public about the "scumbags" that the CF would be killing in Afghanistan,[52] he could lament the decade of darkness, and, when he retired, he could blast the bureaucrats.[53] Yet Harper then chose a series of softer-spoken CDSs in Walt Natynczyk and Tom Lawson, who could still be significant players in the policy process but have been far less vocal. The next CDS, Jon Vance, represents perhaps a realization by Harper that choosing a CDS who is seen as too compliant (Lawson) can also be politically risky.

Of course, the context here is key, and David Mulroney, one of the CF's greatest thorns, recognized that the CF had "the most skin in the game, which gave them more influence."[54] While some civilians were killed and injured in Afghanistan, 158 soldiers died while serving there, and far more were wounded.[55] That kind of risk gave them more sway and made it much harder to micromanage them. The CF resisted Mulroney and Bossenmaier mightily when they sought to coordinate a military that did not want to be coordinated. Ben Rowswell, a DFAIT employee who held the position of RoCK from 2009 to 2010, reported that the military refused to restrict itself to the six priorities and three projects when other objectives and efforts were deemed worthy of the CF's attention.[56] The news out of Iraq in 2015, that the SOF were doing more than

initially expected, raised questions about how much civilian direc-
tion these forces had received and whether they were exceeding
the intent of their commanders. Answers are hard to glean, however, both because these events are quite recent and because CDS
Tom Lawson provided very mixed messages. Again, to be clear,
the deployment to Iraq is quite small and will remain so. Why?
Because civilians will be reluctant to put the CF in a position similar to the one they placed it in, in Kandahar in the near to medium future.[57] Consequently, rather than the military dominating
Canadian foreign policy in the future, Kandahar represents a peak
that is unlikely to be repeated soon, and its enhanced influence is
likely to be only temporary.

The Credibility Problem of Today and Tomorrow

There are good reasons for the CF to consider its efforts in
Afghanistan to be successful. As I discussed in this chapter, it
helped to foster a cultural change within the organization, it improved its status with its international partners, and it changed
how it was regarded in Canada. But the record in Kandahar is de-
cidedly mixed. It may very well be the case that many of the things
that Canada did during its time in Kandahar will dissipate. The
schools may close, the roads may fall into disrepair, and the Taliban may have more than a few successes. So Canadians may won-
der whether it was all worthwhile. I return to this question in the
conclusion of this book, but the point here is that the CF may undermine its current popularity if it continues to act as though
Afghanistan was very successful.

One of the criticisms of the CF during the mission was that its
reports were entirely too optimistic, and this caused problems for
politicians, who had to then explain the failures, such as two major
prison breaks and assassinations of key interlocutors.[58] The CF,
like most militaries, takes seriously the lessons that it can draw
from any operation or mission. It will adapt so that the lessons
learned in blood in Kandahar might mean making different decisions and following new tactics in the next engagement. The junior

officers who served in Afghanistan will be in key decision-making positions in 10 and 20 years. But their influence might be limited by one way in which the CF did not adapt – being overly positive about how things played out in Kandahar.[59] The CF did indeed punch above its weight, but those punches had a limited impact. Its willingness to take risks by delegating to its commanders on the ground was a big improvement as it faced 21st-century problems, but as it looks forward and back, it will need to make honest assessments so that its future judgments can be trusted. Otherwise, it will be ignored as politicians will find its overly optimistic perspectives to be less than useful.

chapter eight

Where Are the Canadians?
The Public and the Media

The oft-repeated mantra "Canadians are confused about Afghanistan" can do much to obscure how well Canadians understood the realities of that country despite the failures of the government and the media to inform them. There were many conflicting dynamics in play both in Afghanistan and in Ottawa, so there was much to distract and obscure. Yet, if we look at the patterns of public opinion over the course of the Kandahar years, we may just find that the public "got it" – Canadians understood that the conflict was difficult, that Canada was working with unreliable individuals (such as the Karzai family), and that progress would be hard to measure.

Thus, the first step here is to figure out what the public thought of the mission. Then we ought to consider the media as it can inform the public or mostly mirror it. Of course, for the most part, the media was merely following Ottawa, so we also need to consider the Canadian government's messaging efforts.

An Ambivalent Public

The Canadian public, after an initial burst of enthusiasm, had essentially mixed opinions about the Afghanistan mission. As Figure 8.1 below illustrates, in the aftermath of 9/11, the Canadian public rallied around the first mission, helping the Americans depose the Taliban and fight Al-Qaeda.

Figure 8.1: Canadian Public Opinion[1]

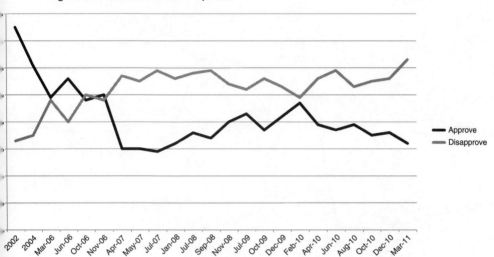

After that, the public supported the mission, by a slight margin, until the end of 2006 and the start of 2007. It is easy to suggest that the mission's popularity dropped as Canadians started to die in greater numbers.[2] However, the patterns are not as clear as that. Figure 8.2 below charts the pattern of public opinion along with the yearly totals of the number of soldiers killed in Afghanistan.[3]

This figure does show that public support dropped at the same time as the first big wave of casualties occurred in 2006.[4] However, it also demonstrates a rebound in support, modest as it was, in 2008 and 2009 even as the casualty totals remained at the same level – about 20 per year. If casualties depress public support, then Canadian opposition to the war should have continued to mount, and support should have collapsed entirely. Instead, after bottoming out near 30 per cent, public support mostly varied around and just below 40 per cent until near the end of the Kandahar deployment. Scholars studying Canadian public opinion have found that there were no simple relationships between the coffins coming home and the public's positions on the war. Indeed, depending on

Figure 8.2: Public Opinion and Casualties

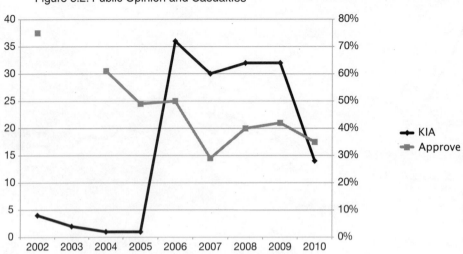

the study, scholars tend to find that public support increased in the short term[5] and that casualties closer to home, especially for Conservative voters, tended to be associated with more support.[6] Regional differences tended to trump other dynamics: no matter what happened, Albertans maintained strong support for the mission, Quebeckers tended to be opposed, and the rest of the country was in between.[7]

Public support was probably shaped by the stances taken by politicians.[8] Efforts by the government to market the mission to the public failed to be sufficiently engaging.[9] The Manley Panel and the extension vote in 2008, which created a temporary sense of elite consensus, may have been responsible for the temporary upswing in support in 2008 and 2009. On the other hand, Harper hid from the war after mid-2008 (see figures 4.1 and 4.2 in Chapter 4), which may have facilitated the dip in support after 2009. It may also be the case that public support did not utterly collapse in 2009–10 precisely because of the commitment to end the Kandahar mission in 2011: with the end in sight, neither supporters nor opponents, perhaps, were compelled to muster much effort to rally for or against the mission.

On the specific issue that captured so much attention – detainees – public opinion was rather nuanced. At the end of 2009, after several years of coverage of the issue, more Canadians found the CF to be credible on this issue than any of the political parties, and it was not even close.[10] Forty-two per cent found the CF to be credible on the detainee issue, but a similar percentage viewed the Conservative government as lacking in credibility. Thus, the public distinguished between an agency of the government – the military – and the government itself. The public was just as dubious of the opposition parties on this issue as it was of the government. Of course, this may be a case of the public supporting the military and scoffing at all politicians, but given the accusations that the military was covering up potential war crimes, the general pattern is still striking.

On the key issue of whether the government passed detainees to the Afghan security forces knowing that they might be tortured, Canadians were divided pretty evenly, with 38 per cent saying yes, 36 per cent saying never, and 26 per cent being unsure.[11] This varied somewhat across the country, but neither proposition received majority support anywhere in Canada, although, again, Quebec and Alberta[12] were mirror images. The next year, a poll indicated that nearly half of Canadians did not follow the detainee story, with 41 per cent following it somewhat closely and only 16 per cent following it very closely.[13] A near majority believed that the process by which documents would be made accessible would not give MPs sufficient information to understand the detainee issue. And that turned out to be rather prescient.

To sum up, the detainee issue seems to be the one dimension of the conflict that received the most media attention during the mission, yet the Canadian public was divided and not as interested as the hothouse environment of Ottawa suggested.[14] Given all of the contradictions and complications, not to mention the elite disagreements, we should not be surprised that the Canadian public did not articulate a clear signal to politicians – except that they preferred the mission in Kandahar to end, which it did.

The Canadian Media at War

Of all parts of the Canadian political system, the element that was perhaps most ready and willing to do what was necessary to succeed was the media. Reporters from a variety of outlets, including television, radio, and newspapers, were willing to risk their lives as they embedded with the CF and the other contingents in Afghanistan.[15] Michelle Lang of the *Calgary Herald* died in December 2009 while she was embedded with the CF, making it very clear that journalists were taking the same risks as the army. Another journalist, Melissa Fung of the CBC, was kidnapped near Kabul in 2008 and was released after 28 days. Graeme Smith, Murray Brewster, Matthew Fisher, Christine Blatchford, and many others accepted these risks and provided many stories that helped to illustrate for Canadians the complexities of Afghanistan and the challenges facing both military and civilian efforts in Kandahar and elsewhere.[16]

The media largely did its job of asking tough questions and investigating claims made by the Canadian military, the Harper government, and NATO. The public viewed the media's handling of the war quite positively, although polls suggested that the media covered combat at the expense of the governance and development efforts.[17] Analyses of the Canadian media indicate that although the outlets depended heavily on government sources, they were still able to contest the government's framing of the issues.[18] The most visible and controversial example of this was Graeme Smith's story about the treatment of detainees who had been transferred from the CF to the Afghan National Security Forces.[19] His story directly contradicted the government's assertions about detainees, spurring debate in Parliament and in Ottawa.

One key problem with the detainee story is that the media lost sight of the greater implications – not that Canadians were possibly involved in war crimes but that the story demonstrated the tremendous challenge faced by Canada and its allies in building any semblance of governance. If the goal was to help foster a self-sustaining Afghan government, the detainee story should have made it clearer to everyone that this goal might just be out of reach.

Another problem with the focus on the detainee story is that it crowded out discussion of other issues in Afghanistan and Canada's engagement. As I said earlier, the detainee story was a serious issue, but it was secondary to the more important questions about the mission itself, the progress reports, and Canada's fixation on Kandahar versus the larger war effort in Afghanistan.

Blame the Government

Public relations personnel working for the government were frustrated that the media seemed to be focused on the bad news, that the "three Ds" did not refer to "democracy, defence, and development" but "deaths, detainees, and denial of information."[20] One could criticize the media for a "if it bleeds, it leads" strategy, but given how hard it was and is to measure progress, it was not surprising that the negative stories tended to resonate more. A key challenge for the media was that the government was quite constrained in its ability to sell the mission. These constraints were partially due to the complexity of the effort but also due to limitations imposed by the government.

Despite putting tremendous effort into communications and messaging, key elements of the government failed to communicate adequately with the Canadian people. A majority of the Canadians surveyed in 2010 said that the government was providing too little information on the war.[21] Indeed, it spent more time and effort hiding from the war than communicating about it and trying to sell it; figures 4.1 and 4.2 in Chapter 4 illustrate Harper's avoidance of the war after 2008. Others have studied this issue more extensively, finding that "members of Harper's cabinet were forbidden to use the word *war*."[22] Boucher finds that Liberal and Conservative governments were particularly silent when it came to casualties, mentioning them only 17 times between September 2001 and September 2009.[23] These omissions fit the larger pattern of restricting media access to the base where bodies were flown in from Afghanistan (Trenton), not lowering flags to half-mast when soldiers were killed, and not attending repatriation ceremonies. Indeed, Harper even told the governor general not to attend the repatriation ceremony in April 2006. "It was better if she did not attend."[24] Some of these decisions were reversed when they faced nearly universal condemnation, although the pattern of the prime minister not attending the repatriation ceremonies continued.[25]

When discussing the war, Canadians will disagree about the goals, making it harder to evaluate what was accomplished. Boucher argues that this is the product of mixed messaging. He performed extensive content analyses to ascertain how the Afghanistan mission had been explained to Canadians and found that there was "significant variation in the quality and content of government speeches on Afghanistan."[26] However, defenders of the government could argue that Boucher's period of study ended in March 2008, just as the government was setting its course of action in the aftermath of the Manley Panel.

Indeed, after the Manley Report was released, public messaging became a key priority of the WG effort. Not only was more attention paid to a website devoted to Canada's engagement in Afghanistan,[27] but much work also went into the quarterly reports sent to Parliament, documenting the progress made. Of course, these reports were part of a larger problem, identified in Chapter 6: the priorities and projects in the WG effort had only tangential relationships with winning the war. Canadians could learn that the progress reports were improving, but they knew that the war was no closer to being won.

A key problem is that most of the actors on the ground in Kandahar faced significant restrictions on communicating with the media.[28] The CF could and would chat with the media, but few civilians other than the RoCK had the authority to talk with the media and go off script.[29] Boudreau suggested in our interview in June 2013 that there was a "long-standing culture of public servants not speaking to the media about what it is they do." There is something to this, but there also seemed to be a culture of fear, which seemed particularly intense. Reporters had little incentive to talk about the development and governance efforts with most of the Canadian civilians in Kandahar since they would either not speak or would refer to the talking points developed in Ottawa.

While the military story might always be more interesting to the media and the Canadian public, the restrictions placed on the civilians made any story about their work boring and not worth many column inches back in Canada.

It is also clear that the government agencies varied quite widely in their ability to deliver their messages, to communicate with attentive audiences. One day of briefings provides an example of the contrasting abilities of the CF and CIDA to engage in messaging. In 2008, the military head of NATO, American General Bantz Craddock, visited Ottawa, and the CF invited a small group of academics (including myself), whom it viewed as opinion leaders,[30] to sit at the same table as the entire Canadian command group (mostly three-star officers) and Craddock as they chatted about the Afghanistan mission. We academics were even allowed to ask tough questions and received rather honest answers. The meeting was off the record, so we could not report what Craddock said, but the event left us all favourably disposed towards the CF leadership for giving us such amazing access and relative candour.

CIDA learned of this event, so it organized a roundtable at its offices, later the same day, with most of the academics who had attended the meeting with Craddock. We, the scholars at this additional roundtable, were flummoxed as the CIDA representatives were far more interested in asking us how they should message better than in giving us any insights into what was going on in Afghanistan. Given that we academics were political scientists who had studied international relations and not journalism professors who had studied public relations, we were the wrong group to be asked how one should message. Indeed, this roundtable itself was poor messaging. The difference displayed that day between the CF and CIDA was night and day in terms of ability to communicate favourably to a sceptical audience.

Conclusion

This chapter addressed two key actors outside the government – the public and the media. What did we learn about Canadians from their reactions to the war? Public support declined as casualties mounted, but we need to be cautious about saying that the public will oppose any mission that places Canadians at risk as the public might have been just as turned off by the other part of the violence dynamic – in which Canadian soldiers were doing the killing too and not just handing out chocolate bars. It is more likely that what really mattered was the partisan politics of the mission. People followed their political parties, so as the Liberals began to oppose the mission they had initiated, more Canadians began to oppose the mission. After that split, public support for the mission stabilized even as casualties mounted. The government's decision in 2008 to leave Afghanistan in 2011 meant that the last three years of combat would produce an exit, something that most parties and much of the public wanted, whether that departure was a result of victory or exhaustion.

The media did its job pretty well: embedded reporters risked their lives and provided critical stories challenging the government's messaging; and the Canadian-based media covered the fights in Parliament, which centred on the detainee issue. The various outlets did not really pursue the hard, long-term questions regarding the conflicts between Kandahar as Canada's focus and the larger war in Afghanistan, and they spent more time on detainees than other issues that were more central. Yet they covered what the government was trying to nuance and finesse, so the media did shine spotlights where they needed to be directed.

The government, despite complaints about the media and a confused public, bears most of the responsibility for the mismanaged messaging. Denials, distractions, and diversions were a disservice to the public and made the jobs of officials that much harder. More clarity at the outset of each story would have removed much of the kindling for the media fires that developed. Instead, denials just encouraged the opposition and the media to pursue these stories further. The government also lacked the trust it should have had in its civilian operatives in the field. If they had been given the green light to talk about their work, the reporters down range would have had something to cover other than the CF's efforts and the coffins flowing home.

In any endeavour like this, mistakes will be made. The question is whether to own them or deny them. This government chose to deny, which undermined its credibility and gave the opposition easy targets. The Canadian public could and did understand that this war was difficult. If the government had trusted the public more and the media as well, it might have been able to send clearer messages and delay the inevitable decline in support. There is much that we can learn from the Afghanistan experience, and a key lesson of this chapter is that the public was not as confused or as immature as some have argued. Indeed, if the messaging around Afghanistan said anything, it was that the government of Canada was not ready for such a tough mission and preferred not to talk about it.

chapter nine

Learning Lessons and Drawing Conclusions

Any evaluation of Canada's foreign and defence policy institutions that uses the Afghanistan experience as a test must take seriously the fact that it was an incredibly difficult mission in a uniquely challenging place. To try to build a self-sustaining government is hard under any conditions, let alone in one of the poorest countries in the world and one that has been through more than 20 years of war. With neighbours competing to undermine the effort, with Afghanistan's leaders far more interested in their own wealth and welfare than the common good, and with allies that had conflicting ways of operating, there was only so much that Canada could do.

In the grand scheme of things, Canada could have performed far worse. Despite the focus on detainees, there was no episode like the Somalia Affair. For Canada, there was no event like the Kunduz bombing, in which German mistakes led to an American plane killing over 100 civilians.[1] While the projects Canada funded and oversaw may not lead to sustainable improvements, thus far there have been no news stories about hundreds of millions of dollars spent on military headquarters that were never needed.[2] Although the toll Canada suffered was awful – more than 160 Canadian lives lost,[3] with many more wounded and suffering post-traumatic stress syndrome – it could have been a lot worse. Canadian soldiers were operating on roads seeded with landmines, among populations where suicide bombers could easily hide, and frequently came under fire from machine guns and rocket-propelled grenades. They were definitely in harm's way, but due to their equipment, their training, the poor marksmanship of the adversary, and other factors, the CF dodged far more bullets and bombs than one might have expected.

On the other hand, Canada could have performed better, as could the rest of NATO, its partners, and the Afghan government. There could have been far more coordination among the disparate actors to avoid duplicating and undermining the efforts of the other nations. There could have been more strategic consistency, fewer prison breaks, better messaging with greater transparency. There might have been more media coverage of the less kinetic sides of the operation had more of the civilians on the ground been allowed to talk to the press. The military might have had more credibility if it had not been so relentlessly optimistic in public.

In this concluding chapter, I try to evaluate how the various elements of Canadian politics performed relatively – which parts were ready for this kind of effort, which ones adapted well, which ones adapted poorly, which ones failed to adjust at all. In this process, I will try to identify lessons that can be learned about how Canada operates when it engages in a multidimensional effort abroad. I will also address a question that I have often been asked and that all Canadians need to answer for themselves: was this worth it? To preview my answer below, it depends on what one means by the question. By considering the individual words "this," "worth," and "it," I will ultimately conclude that the Canadian mission in Afghanistan was indeed worthwhile in the end.

Variations in Adaptation

The first lesson to be learned is that we cannot rely on government to learn lessons. Or, to put it another way, we cannot rely on government to share the lessons that they have learned. In the course of researching this book and networking in Ottawa, I had numerous conversations with individuals working in the government. More than a few mentioned that there was an ongoing effort to engage in a real lessons-learned exercise so that Canada could do this kind of thing better the next time.[4] This would be really good news if the government understood Step 3 of any lessons-learned exercise: once you do all of the research, and after you write up the analyses, you need to disseminate the results. Instead, a document that could shed a lot of light on this important experience is sitting on a shelf somewhere. My attempt to obtain it through an Access to Information request was denied.[5] The problem is not that I am not able to obtain this lessons-learned document, but that *no one* can. This means that the various government agencies are less likely to work out how to do better next time. Thus, it is up to others to assess what can be learned and then spread the word so that people in and near government might determine what to avoid and what to do the next time Canada engages in a serious international effort.[6]

As I discussed at the outset, Canada was not really ready for a combat-intensive, multidimensional counter-insurgency effort in a difficult place. To be fair, none of the allies were ready for the challenging war in Afghanistan (although some were better prepared), but the focus here is on Canada. Each element of Canada's political system – from the politicians to the military to the other government agencies to the public and the media – had to learn and adapt as Afghanistan presented them all with difficult choices and challenging battlefields. Some adapted, and some did not. Below, I suggest which actors learned what and whether they adapted along the way. To be clear, not all adaptations are progressive.

Immature Politicians

The politicians clearly were not ready. They were in a position where they had to make very hard decisions but did not know how to handle the consequences of those decisions. Paul Martin, with significant alliance pressure, chose to send troops to Kandahar and has run away from that decision ever since. I cannot help but think that the Liberal Party has lost a lot of its credibility on foreign policy issues for opposing a mission that it started. The reasons given – rotation schemes, other peacekeeping possibilities, whatever – are numerous but utterly unconvincing. In hindsight, the

Liberals should have focused on the disjunction between what they had started and what was actually going on in the field. For instance, they made the decision to send the CF in and set up a PRT in Kandahar, but they fell short of actually assessing how this effort was going. They could have focused on improving coordination between Canada and NATO, an obvious weakness and an issue that played to the heart of the Liberal ideology of multilateralism. Instead of being distracted by the detainee issue, the Liberals could have focused on whether the CF's quarterly reports reflected the realities and whether they had anything to do with winning the war. There were many opportunities to focus on the big questions. Instead, the Liberals took the easy way out, consistently shifting focus to issues that were secondary but that may have seemed more salient to public perception.[7]

Stephen Harper proved to be most adaptable as he developed new strategies to gain support from the Liberals in order to share responsibility for the mission – the pop quiz–like first extension vote in 2006 and then the Manley Panel. He was under no real obligation to obtain extension votes, but doing so allowed him to launder accountability.[8] This was an interesting lesson to learn but not a progressive one. Indeed, not very long after the 2008 extension decision, Harper shied away from discussing the mission. He stopped speaking about it and imposed strict message control on nearly every Canadian official working in or on the Afghanistan effort. This was hardly a helpful move as it meant that the media could cover only the military effort (complete with ramp ceremonies) and the spats in Ottawa. Perhaps it worked politically as he did eventually receive the coveted parliamentary majority in 2011. However, it failed in that it made it harder for Canadians to glean a full picture of the war. In other countries, politicians stood in front of their war effort despite significant costs – the Danes paid a higher price per capita, yet their politicians continued to explain and justify their involvement in the war, and their public support did not drop as quickly.[9]

To sum up, there were lessons learned by politicians, but I would argue that they were the wrong lessons. By frequently denying responsibility or refusing to discuss the mission, the nation's leaders

failed to lead Canadians, providing ample room for mispercep-
tions and myths to generate. Perhaps I have heroic assumptions
about politics, but I tend to think that parties abandon responsibility at their peril.

The Limits of Parliament and Canada's Political Parties

As should be clear from the discussion in Chapter 5, Parliament
and the various players in it performed as poorly as the nation's
leaders. By choosing to focus on the matter of detainees, parliamentarians drew attention away from much larger and more important matters pertaining to the mission. Not only that, but at the
end of the day, not much was accomplished as a result of this, in
my view, misdirected concentration.

The problems here are both institutional and political. The
Canadian legislature lacks the tools it needs to engage in serious
oversight, whether it be over the military or over the minister responsible for the military. The relevant committees do not have
security clearances, the members do not have sufficient expertise,
and they do not have staff with sufficient experience. As a result,
they do not know what questions to ask, have to rely on selectively leaked documents,[10] and have limited ability to hold anyone accountable. Of course, even if such tools and expertise
existed, they would be useful only if the political parties took the
issues seriously rather than as part of the gamesmanship of partisan politics. The public could then derive a decent sense of whether questions and investigations were largely aimed at scoring
points or at improving Canada's performance in Afghanistan. The
detainee issue served a number of purposes simultaneously, giving one side the ability to score points at the expense of the others.
Other issues might have been far more important for Canada's
interests in terms of achieving success and reducing costs in
Afghanistan, but they did not have the simplicity or the appeal of
accusing someone of being a war criminal or a fellow traveller of
the Taliban.

The irony here is that Parliament did detect a problem and came
close to innovating: the special committee set up to vet the detainee documents was an attempt to bridge the information gap. But it

was a temporary, constricted bandage, when what was needed was a real empowering of the various committees that dealt with the ministers who were overseeing the secret stuff. The Defence Committee should consist of both parliamentarians and staff with security clearances so that they can hold closed meetings to which they can call the minister (and lower-level staff) and put his or her feet to the fire. While this would make it difficult for the MPs involved to divulge secrets to the press, it might just cause the minister and the military to anticipate such events and avoid doing things that lead to such hearings.[11] Indeed, one of the basic problems in the Canadian government is that it denies that something is wrong until it becomes entirely unsustainable. Had parliamentarians been equipped with more expertise and more information, they may have found out that there was more smoke than fire on the detainee file, and the government's agencies might have been more willing to acknowledge the problems.

There are problems with this approach, as others have documented.[12] However, the process of holding the minister to account fails when parliamentarians lack the information they need to understand what questions they should be asking, let alone to get the answers they need. The New Democrats have showed on other issues, namely the F-35 file, that if they develop enough knowledge, they can put the government in legitimately tough spots. That is, by doing the job really well, they can hold the government to account and score political points.

In the case of Afghanistan, Parliament was almost entirely irrelevant. Some might argue that this is a good thing, but it is dangerous for good civilian control of the military if only a small coterie within the government knows what is really going on. Not everyone needs to know everything about what the military and others on the ground are doing, but most would agree that the "circle of trust" needs to be widened beyond just the prime minister and the minister of national defence.

Whole of Government

As I have attempted to show in this book, convincing the various Canadian agencies to cooperate was perhaps one of the greatest sources of stress off the actual battlefield. Clearly, at the start, the agencies were not prepared for the kind of effort they would be facing in Kandahar, let alone being ready to play well with the other agencies involved.

CIDA had a great deal of experience in doing long-term development, which focused on cooperating with international institutions, NGOs, and national capitals. But it had little experience in doing short-term development, working with the CF, or operating in a combat zone. Its centralized processes were perhaps well suited for normal situations, but they were poorly suited to being agile in Afghanistan. CIDA's record is, ultimately, mixed. It did pour significant resources into Kandahar when persuaded by those running the WG effort, but it could not understand how to communicate its efforts to the Canadian public. Now that CIDA has been merged with DFAIT to form the Department of Foreign Affairs, Trade and Development, the question is whether CIDA's legacies will dominate future development efforts in conflict zones or be replaced by DFAIT's tendencies.

DFAIT may have made the greatest progress of all. Going into Afghanistan, it had little experience in governance work, working with local and regional politicians to coordinate the many different efforts involving the rest of the Canadian government's presence in Kandahar. The innovation of the RoCK and the creation of a Cabinet-level position were key adaptations. The series of RoCKs had more authority to make decisions on the ground, although they were perhaps too tied to the inflexible metrics developed in Ottawa – the six priorities and three signature projects.

This brings us to a key problem with the effort. The main tool, the centrally defined and measured priorities aimed at providing coherence to the Canadian effort in Afghanistan, was focused on satisfying the political actors in Ottawa and not on winning the war in Afghanistan. This is perhaps unavoidable as the main tool Mulroney and then Bossenmaier had to force recalcitrant agencies to cooperate was not reminding them what was best for winning the war but referring to the mandate set down by the prime minister and the parliamentary extension vote. In the future, it will be up to the political masters more than the public servants to keep the focus on the larger goals of the effort.

This leads to a second challenge: it is hard to adapt and remain consistent at the same time. One of the basic tensions between DFAIT and CIDA on the one hand and the CF on the other was that the latter was much more willing to adapt to the changing circumstances on the ground, but adaptations risked reducing consistency. The way to deal with this was to focus on *coherence* rather than *consistency*. Doing the same thing despite changes on the ground may have been consistent, but, of course, it could be dysfunctional as well. If all of the Canadian government had adapted at roughly the same rate to the events on the ground, the effort could have remained coherent. Of course, this would have imposed an obligation on the government to explain to the public why changes were being made. Keeping to the original plan (six priorities, three projects) made it possible to tell a simple story but also meant that Canada was not adapting to changing circumstances.

How does Canada maintain coherence while adapting? Perhaps the most important move would be to have the various government agencies involved in the effort become more similar in how they delegate discretion to the people on the ground. Coherence was always going to be problematic for Canada, with one agency making all of its decisions in Ottawa (CIDA), another delegating a lot of discretion to its commanders in the field (the CF), and the third (DFAIT) in between. When the Canadian military commander in Kandahar wanted to revise his plans – whether to conform more closely to events in the province or work better with NATO allies – he had the power to do so. This was not the case for most of the other Canadian actors in Afghanistan, which meant that coherence was always at risk. If the RoCK had been empowered to revise its priorities in coordination with the CF commander and the other civilians on the ground, Canada's effort could have remained coherent. The alternative would have been to have all decisions made in Ottawa – that too would have improved Canadian coherence, although at the risk of decreasing coordination with the rest of ISAF. Instead, given the widespread nature of decision-making powers, incoherence was endemic to the Canadian approach from start to finish.

The next time Canada engages in a complex foreign operation, coordinators will need to pay attention to how the various organizations manage and communicate about distant efforts. It is perhaps wishful thinking, but if the various agencies grant similar levels of discretion, all of the actors in the field will be more likely to be on the same page. During the Afghanistan mission, creating positions at the top and the bottom to manage the civilian efforts – the deputy minister and the RoCK – was a key innovation that finessed this problem to a degree, and one lesson of this mission is that such adaptations should be deployed the next time. The problem, of course, is that the power of the deputy minister in any effort is directly related to the interest of the prime minister; once that dissipates, the deputy minister position loses much of its heft and relevance.[13]

The Canadian Forces: Firm and Flexible

When I started researching the Afghanistan mission, one of the first interviews I had with a Canadian officer, Brigadier-General David Fraser, turned into a lecture on "effects-based operations."[14] Fraser, who had commanded during Operation Medusa, wanted to explain to me how every effort in Afghanistan had to focus on not just winning a battle but also whether the desired effects had been achieved in the short, medium, and long runs. The irony of this new doctrine is that the CF was probably far more effective in having a lasting impact in Canada than in Afghanistan. In Kandahar, until ISAF forces were reinforced by the American surge, most of the fighting, aside from keeping Kandahar City in the hands of the government, had a temporary impact. The CF was considered to be engaged in either lawn-mowing or acting as a fire brigade. Both analogies reflect how temporary a battlefield victory would be. Operation Medusa testifies to this as it did not cement control over that part of the province in the long term.

On the other hand, there seemed to be a clear interest within the Canadian forces to use their efforts in Afghanistan to change their image from that of peacekeepers to one of warriors. On this point, one must concede that the result was successful, even as we dispel the myth that the CF manipulated public opinion in the interest of deploying to Kandahar (see Chapter 3). The very fact that the myth exists, however, speaks to a larger problem, alluded to earlier: that the relentless optimism about progress on the ground created high expectations, which, in turn, posed challenges not just for the civilians back home but for the CF itself down the road. Every setback in Afghanistan, when measured against the optimistic statements regularly circulated by the CF, could not help but foster cynicism about its intentions or competence in future missions. I myself do not believe that the CF is incompetent or prone to lying to the public, but the discrepancy between what was being said and the reality on the ground raised questions about the CF's credibility.

Maintaining morale in spite of bleak circumstances is an unavoidable and fundamental challenge for any military. Even now, one will not hear the CF utter the word "failure," whereas civilians in other parts of the government use that word to describe Afghanistan.[15] Perhaps the CF can see Kandahar as a success because it did not lose individual battles, because it held onto the city, and because it made a difference while it was there.

The real test, of course, will be the next few years. Will the training effort from 2011 to 2014, combined with the previous years of mentoring in Kandahar, pay off with a stable and functional Afghan military? If so, then the CF's effort can be considered a success. Moreover, much of what may cause Afghanistan to fail was far outside the realm of the military – Pakistan's support for the insurgents, President Karzai's opposition to real institution building, the deep corruption that the international presence could only exacerbate, the incoherence of the NATO effort, and the fickleness of American efforts in the country. Given the many challenges it had to work around, the CF did an amazingly commendable job in what it was supposed to do.

Of all parts of the Canadian government, the CF performed the best in adjusting to the actual circumstances of the mission. It may not have been ready at the outset, but it adapted both old and new technologies and tactics for this unique battlefield. Although it had just recently rejected the use of tanks, the CF realized that it could deploy them against the challenges of the rural battlefield – clay walls and grape-drying huts that resisted smaller arms. So it innovated by leasing tanks from NATO partners. Similarly, when the Manley Panel reported that the CF needed helicopters and unmanned aerial vehicles, the CF quickly found ways to move such equipment onto the battlefield to reduce the risks facing convoys and reduce the number of casualties. Some adaptations may not have been as helpful – such as sending relatively junior officers to WG meetings to limit the influence of the civilians. Overall, though, the CF faced the toughest challenges, paid the highest price, and managed to do pretty well under difficult circumstances. It changed its reputation both at home and abroad, going from being "Can'tbats" to among the most reliable forces in NATO.

The Public and the Media

To say that Canadians were confused is not really a criticism. Afghanistan, after all, is a confusing place, COIN is far more opaque than conventional war, and the politicians in Ottawa did a poor job of communicating to the public. Studies have shown that Canadians are not as averse to risk or casualties as is often supposed (see Chapter 8). At first, when the politicians were united on the subject, the public largely supported the mission; it reduced its support only when dissension crept into the political ranks. The public did not send a clear signal on the detainee scandal as much scepticism was aimed at most of the actors involved, especially the political parties. To me, this reflects a mature public, one that did not jump to any conclusions about this particular matter or about other issues during the war.

   To be sure, the public's attention may have waxed and waned, but that had as much to do with the media's attention span and the politicians' strategies as the public's own fatigue. Indeed, the public remains engaged. Over the past couple of years, I have both presented at and attended numerous events on Afghanistan, and there is still an attentive Canadian public interested in what Canada did, what lasting impact it had, and where Afghanistan will go from here. To be certain of this, more polls will need to be conducted to ascertain longer-lasting attitudes and assessments. Moreover, scholars will need to carry out some comparative analysis because – dare I say it – the Canadian public was probably not that different from the public in any other NATO country.

The media as a whole did rather well. It did not hesitate to send reporters into harm's way in order to develop an accurate picture of what was happening, it covered the hearings in Ottawa intensively, and it sought outside expertise on a regular basis. Most news outlets tended to focus more on the military side of things than on governance and development efforts, but this was for reasons other than the conventional trope that "if it bleeds, it leads." CF personnel were far more open than others, enabling reporters to file more interesting stories. Canada's greatest investment was also on the military side, so it made sense to focus on that. And, yes, it made for better visuals and more compelling stories compared to the complexities of aid workers dealing with a corrupt government, weak institutions, long-term projects, and thoroughly vetted talking points.

Of course, the media could have done more had the government been more cooperative. The rules imposed on non-CF officials sent into the field, as well as the fear generated back home by a message-controlling government, limited the number of sources and access overall. This brings us back to what was said at the outset of the chapter: that there are valuable lessons to be learned if only the government would show itself less averse to criticism. With a mission as long and complicated as Afghanistan, mistakes were sure to be made – both major and minor. Refusing to accept that reality, because the government fears losing control of messaging, does a real disservice to future efforts and to Canadians in general.

Was It Worth It?

The debate about whether the mission was worth it is well underway.[16] A total of 158 Canadian soldiers and a handful of civilians died in this effort. Canada spent billions of dollars on both aid and the military effort, and they were the focal point of the entire foreign and defence apparatus of the country for the better part of a decade. Given the sacrifices made by the soldiers and others deployed to Afghanistan, as well as the financial costs incurred by the Canadian taxpayers, it is incumbent upon the government, the media, the public, and those who study these matters to consider whether the effort was worth it. The Canadian public, 10 years after 9/11 and following the CF's withdrawal from Kandahar, did not think the war was worthwhile.[17]

To approach the question of whether the mission was worthwhile, we need to be clear about what it was that Canada was trying to do. If Canada deployed troops to Afghanistan to build a self-sustaining, stable, secure democracy, then it is likely to be the case that the mission failed.[18] It is still too soon to judge as we do not know what will happen now that Hamid Karzai is no longer president and most of NATO has left the country.[19] However, several signs point to a less stable, less secure, and less democratic Afghanistan. There is more violence now than when Canada deployed. The rehabilitation of the Dahla Dam is not complete, although irrigation has improved. The investments made in schools may not pay off as officials have already shown an inability to sustain their part of the effort to keep teachers at these schools. The only thing we can be sure of is that the individuals who received polio vaccinations will not contract polio. This is not to say that there has been no progress at all in Kandahar, just that whatever progress has been made may not continue with far fewer foreign troops in the country.

The six priorities and three signature projects (see Chapter 6) were an effort by the WG team to provide focus and consistency, but they can be deceptive as they were really justifications for the mission rather than predetermined reasons for Canada's engagement. As I argued earlier in the book, Canada did not go to Afghanistan to turn it into a democracy that respected human rights and fostered functioning institutions. It went to Afghanistan because an ally was attacked and a key multilateral institution became involved. This effort was consistent both with Canada's past and with what its allies were doing. Canada has made military commitments to every NATO effort, from defending western Europe from a possible Soviet invasion to Bosnia to Kosovo to Afghanistan to Libya, and, most recently, to Ukraine and the Baltics. Similarly, every NATO country showed up to some degree (unlike the case of Libya), and non-NATO countries that otherwise have alliances and ties to the United States made serious commitments as well (such as Australia and New Zealand).

Taking all this into consideration, I think a better approach to the question "Was it worth it?" is to think about whether the relationship with the United States and membership in NATO were worth the casualties and financial commitment. It comes down to both interests and values[20] as working with the United States and NATO makes sense both from the standpoint of Canada's national security interests and from the perspective of Canadian values. In terms of interests, Canada must work with others to maximize its own security; while threats may be distant, Canada lacks the capability to deal with most of these by itself. Working with the United States and working with NATO are basic requirements for Canadian national security. Fulfilling treaty obligations (NATO's Article V) is in Canada's interests, just as it would want other countries to fulfil their obligations to Canada. In terms of values, Canadians believe that their country should make a difference in the world and that it should do so through multilateralism. Working together with other countries is a basic shared value. So even though the efforts in Afghanistan may not be sustained after NATO leaves, making a difference in one spot and working within international institutions to do so is actually quite Canadian. That is what Paul Martin believed in 2005, when he decided to send Canadian troops and civilians to Kandahar.

Canada gained and exerted influence in Afghanistan due to this investment. Its willingness to do the hard work gave it heft within NATO and in Kabul. This effort may or may not pay off in the long run in Afghanistan, but it was an investment in Brussels, Washington, Paris, Germany, London, and elsewhere. Over 160 lives is a high price to pay for gains that are not so tangible; however, militaries are generally thought of as tools of countries as they try to shape international relations. When such tools are used, people pay the price, but those who join the military understand that their role is to be an instrument of national policy.

We can cloud the issue by talking about schools, vaccinations, and the like, but the reality is that Canadian leaders (three of them, from two political parties) sent troops into harm's way because of Canada's place in the world. We can look at the conflicting progress reports about what was achieved in Afghanistan, but the mission always was about Canada's commitment to its allies. Just as

Canada had participated in previous NATO efforts, it engaged in a serious effort in Afghanistan in order to honour this commitment and support its allies. Some might consider this to be placating the United States, but it is more than that. Sending troops to Afghanistan (and to Kandahar in particular) was consistent with Canadian interests and values. From this perspective, therefore, one must conclude that the Afghanistan mission was worth it insofar as it constituted significant support for the most important multilateral security organization and its most important ally.

A Next Time

The basic premise of this book is that we need to reflect on and understand how Canada operated at home and in Afghanistan so that we are better prepared next time. Of course, some will argue that there may not be a next time. Stephen Harper learned his lesson, and NATO too learned a lesson: not to do this again. Indeed, Robert Gates, former US secretary of defence, said that anyone suggesting that the United States become involved in yet another land war in the Middle East should have his or her head examined. There is much to this. The Libya mission, with the mantra of "no boots on the ground," clearly applied lessons learned in Afghanistan as NATO engaged efforts only in the skies above and the waters off Libya. While some SOF participated, there was no intent to engage in any kind of nation-building effort. This has not been good for Libya or its neighbourhood. As this chapter is being written, NATO and its members remain most reluctant to intervene in Syria, while some have contributed air power and training forces to Iraq's fight against the Islamic State.

Yet two basic truths remain: politicians change, and the international system imposes. The first truth is that today's politicians will be replaced by those who have not been as badly burned by Afghanistan, Iraq, or other interventions. Also, politicians change their minds. The Bush administration came into power vowing not to do any of that peace-building, nation-building stuff that had so occupied the Clinton administration in Bosnia and Kosovo. That stance certainly affected how the Bush administration dealt with

Iraq and Afghanistan, but it was ultimately discarded when the United States was faced with broken regimes and a requirement to do something to reduce the chaos.

This speaks to the second enduring reality: that countries' agendas are often not set in their national capitals but elsewhere. In the realm of foreign policy, events have a way of sucking countries into things that they did not seek to undertake. Canada, if it remains a member of NATO, and/or if subsequent political parties buy into the norm of the Responsibility to Protect, will be called upon to participate in another significant military operation. Canada's politicians will face difficult choices as declining to participate may be counter to the country's interests and values, and they will ask the CF whether it can handle the new mission. The CF officers will almost surely reply, "Yes, we can," even if they are not fully ready. That is the way they are trained and socialized – the military is a "can-do" organization. Thus, there will come a time when Canada is asked to do something that is not easy, its politicians will face competing pressures at home and abroad, and its military will not try to veto the effort.

So, yes, there will be a next time. We do not know where, when, or how. It will probably not take the form of a COIN campaign like Afghanistan, but it may not be very different either. Weak and failing states remain a problem. There are still countries whose governments continue to fail their citizens. The plight of refugees fleeing Syria in the latter half of 2015 may ultimately produce a more extensive intervention.[21] There will be more environmental disasters, with political dynamics attached. The world remains a challenging place, and Canadians continue to feel that they have a role in making a difference. They made a difference for a time in Afghanistan, regardless of whether the progress made was sustainable. The question is not whether there will be a next time but when, and whether Canada will be ready for it. As I have tried to demonstrate in this book, parts of Canada – such as the public, the media, and the military – will be prepared for such an eventuality, while others will not. What remains is to reflect on and understand the challenges and outcomes of the Afghanistan mission and to apply those hard-earned, valuable lessons to future efforts around the world.

Notes

Chapter One

1   Canada's combat mission started in late 2001, when Joint Task Force 2 was deployed. Canadian snipers played a key role in 2002 in support of Operation Anaconda.

2   After the merger with CIDA in 2013, DFAIT became the Department of Foreign Affairs, Trade and Development, or DFATD. After the election of the Liberals in 2015, the name of the department changed again to Global Affairs Canada. Since the events of this book predate the merger and the election, I will use *DFAIT*.

3   The website iCasualties.org tracks the individuals killed in action in Iraq and Afghanistan in Operation Iraqi Freedom, in Operation Enduring Freedom, and with the International Security Assistance Force. This total of killed in Afghanistan includes 158 CF personnel listed as killed (even as it includes one dying of natural causes while on leave and two suicides), a senior DFAIT official, a Canadian journalist, and two CIDA contractors. There are widely varying estimates of what the Afghanistan mission has and will cost Canada, with the government stating and analysts suggesting over $20 billion, including the legacy costs of veterans' care down the road; see *Ottawa Citizen*, "Afghan War Costs $22B, So Far: Study," posted on canada.com (website), 18 September 2008, http://www.canada.com/ottawacitizen/news/story.html?id=a6e5f168-2417-4184-abfd-375fec9d4ef3, accessed 21 November 2013. The Canadian government estimated the cost to be $11.3 billion from 2001 to 2011, but that figure did not include future medical costs; see http://www.afghanistan.gc.ca/canada-afghanistan/news-nouvelles/2010/2010_07_09.aspx, accessed 21 November 2013. The *Ottawa Citizen* presented a range of estimates as of February 2014, from $11.3 billion by

the government; $18.1 billion by Kevin Page, the former parliamentary budget officer; and $22 billion by David Perry, a defence analyst; see *Ottawa Citizen*, "Afghanistan by the Numbers," 15 February 2014, B3.

4 For instance, see Brewster 2011; Stein and Lang 2007.

5 For a sample, see Wattie 2008; Conrad 2009; Horn 2010; Patterson and Warren 2008; Windsor and Charters 2008; Wiss 2010; Flavelle 2013. There are also now movies covering the Canadian experience including the fictional *Hyena Road* and the documentary *Kandahar Journals*.

6 Military historian Sean Maloney has written several books covering the first two and a half phases of the war; see Maloney 2005, 2009, 2013a.

7 Friscolanti 2006. See also Corbett 2012.

8 Different rules apparently applied to the snipers, who made quite a name for themselves by providing significant support to American operations, including Operation Anaconda; see Scott Taylor, "'Soldier of Fortune' Lauds Canadian Snipers," *Halifax Herald*, 15 July 2002. This support included the longest successful shot on record until it was exceeded by a British sniper seven years later.

9 Interview with Colonel (ret.) Pat Stogran (vice-president, Pearson Peacekeeping Centre), 25 April 2007, Ottawa.

10 The post–July 2011 training mission was "Kabul-centric," with most of the trainers in and near Kabul but some in Herat and Mazeer-e-Sharif. The numbers used to build this figure come from NATO "placemats" (http://www.isaf.nato.int/isaf-placemat-archives.html, accessed 24 October 2011), presentations given by Canadian officers over the years, and newspaper accounts of the new training mission.

11 Fitzsimmons 2013.

12 This would be repeated by Lieutenant-General Charles Bouchard during the Libyan mission in 2011.

13 The mission in Iraq in 2014–5 is exceptional as it has been far more public than previous Canadian SOF missions.

14 This book focuses almost entirely on the army. The navy had no role to play in landlocked Afghanistan, and the air force played only a supporting role. The efforts and risks were borne almost entirely by the army.

Chapter Two

1 Auerswald and Saideman 2014.

2 The fatality figures are from the iCasualties.org website, using the total as of 10 October 2014. It includes the members of the coalition's armed forces who were killed in action and in accidents and who committed suicide; it does not include civilians. The Canadian number includes non-combat

fatalities, but I use it both here and elsewhere in the text as that is the number most often cited in the media and in popular accounts. Further, it is the number that is most comparable to those listed by other countries, and since the point here is to show the relative burden sharing, it makes sense to use comparable numbers. The maximum size of the contingent is derived from the "placemats" regularly issued by NATO; see http://www.isaf.nato.int/isaf-placemat-archives.html, accessed 21 November 2013. Population statistics are from Eurostat, the Albanian Institute of Statistics (http://www.instat.gov.al), and US and Canadian census figures.

3 Interview with Dutch officer, January 2011, The Hague.

4 Larry Shaughnessy, "One Soldier, One Year: $850,000 and Rising," *Security Clearance* (blog), CNN online, 12 February 2012, http://security.blogs.cnn.com/2012/02/28/one-soldier-one-year-850000-and-rising/, accessed 12 December 2013.

5 See Auerswald and Saideman 2014.

6 Alexander Szandar, "Snafu in Afghanistan: German Troops Bemoan 'Critical' Deficits in Training and Equipment," *Spiegel* Online, 31 August 2009, http://www.spiegel.de/international/world/snafu-in-afghanistan-german-troops-bemoan-critical-deficits-in-training-and-equipment-a-646085.html, accessed 12 December 2013.

7 In French, NATO's other official language, the acronym is ELMO.

8 This was a major complaint that I heard at the Ministry of Rural Reconstruction and Development during a tour in December 2007.

9 Interview with senior French Joint Staff officer, June 2009, Paris.

10 Thompson explained this event during a briefing he gave at McGill University in Montreal, after his tour in Afghanistan, 24 March 2009.

11 For examples, see Naureen Shah, "Don't Deliver Afghans to Torture on a Promise Alone," *The Age* (website), 7 January 2011, http://www.theage.com.au/opinion/politics/dont-deliver-afghans-to-torture-on-a-promise-alone-20110107-19ien.html, accessed 27 March 2013; and Ian Cobain, "British Military under Pressure over Afghan Prisoners," *Guardian* (London), 9 May 2012, http://www.guardian.co.uk/world/2012/may/09/british-military-pressure-afghan-prisoners, accessed 27 March 2013.

12 Indeed, Canada had such a facility in Kandahar, which I toured in December 2007.

13 Interview with official at SHAPE, February 2011, Mons, Belgium.

14 When I served on the Bosnia desk of the US Joint Staff in 2001, there were still empty spots on the master spreadsheet (Combined Joint Statement of Requirements) six years after the NATO mission had begun there.

15 This list omits smaller, non-NATO participants, including Armenia, Azerbaijan, El Salvador, Finland, Ireland, Macedonia, Malaysia, Mongolia,

Montenegro, Singapore, Tonga, Ukraine, and the United Arab Emirates; see http://www.isaf.nato.int/images/stories/File/Placemats/ISAF-ANA%20Troops%20Placemat-Feb19%202013.pdf, accessed 1 March 2013.

16 See Auerswald and Saideman 2014, which explains how and why countries varied in using these mechanisms.

17 This vote and outcome may have been more of an opportunity to collapse the government than about the mission itself.

18 Kreps 2010.

19 Mueller 1973; Baum 2002.

20 Manley et al. 2008.

21 One can debate whether the weakness of Westminster parliaments is due to the institutions themselves or the unwillingness of parliamentarians to impose their will on their governments. Comparing the powers and roles of legislatures and legislators among the world's democracies is my next project.

22 To be clear, as I discuss in the next chapter, I do not think that the CF duped civilians into going to war in order to change its identity, but rather that the Afghanistan conflict, once engaged, proved to be an opportunity for the CF to promote its preferred identity at the expense of the peacekeeping identity.

Chapter Three

1 For an account largely compatible with the one given here, see Matthew Willis, "An Unexpected War, A Not-Unexpected Mission: The Origins of Kandahar 2005," OpenCanada.org, 8 January 2013, http://opencanada .org/features/the-think-tank/essays/an-unexpected-war-a-not-unexpected-mission/, accessed 12 April 2013. See also Bercuson and Granatstein 2011.

2 Interview with former deputy prime minister John Manley, 22 August 2013, Ottawa. Stein and Lang (2007) raise this possibility before presenting their argument.

3 Martin 2009, 394.

4 Stein and Lang 2007.

5 Ibid., 188.

6 Martin 2009, 330. This does provide some clues as to why Canada sent too few troops, which was a mistake made by the rest of the alliance too, as I discussed in Chapter 2.

7 Interview with former prime minister Paul Martin, 29 March 2007, Montreal. I was at an event in Europe in mid-2015 at which former minister of defence Bill Graham repeated the rotation myth.

8 Stein and Lang 2007, 180.
9 In my interview with Paul Martin, he acknowledged that Darfur would have to be a NATO mission, yet it was clear at the time that NATO would not be going to Darfur. Indeed, to send a NATO mission to Darfur would perhaps have required the same kind of persuasion that Serbia had needed to allow NATO into Kosovo – an extended bombing campaign.
10 Martin 2009, 392–3.
11 He has made his Africa focus clear in his statements since, and he did so many times in my interview with him.
12 Interviews with Chris Alexander (former ambassador to Afghanistan), 24 July 2013 (by telephone); Wendy Gilmour (former director general, DFAIT), 15 August 2013, Ottawa; and David Mulroney (former deputy minister, DFAIT), 18 July 2013 (by telephone).
13 See Marten 2010 for a similar discussion.
14 For the term "strategic backwater," see Willis, "An Unexpected War."
15 Christopher Alexander, quoted in Stein and Lang 2007, 133. He reiterated this in my interview with him.
16 Bercuson and Granatstein 2011, 22.
17 For a more academic take, and one that places the Kandahar mission squarely in Canada's national interests, see Massie 2013. The initial decision to go to Kandahar in 2002 was shaped by the same considerations (Sjolander 2009) despite Martin's fundamental desire to distance himself from Jean Chrétien.
18 Stein and Lang 2007, 181.
19 See the relevant sections of Auerswald and Saideman 2014.
20 Willis, "An Unexpected War." See also Zyla 2013.
21 Auerswald and Saideman 2014.
22 For more on the centrality of NATO in Canada's "Atlanticist strategic culture," see Haglund 1997; Jockel and Sokolsky 2009; Massie 2009; Nossal 2004.
23 In my interview with Paul Martin, he noted that both his father, Paul Martin Sr., and Lester B. Pearson had played a role in NATO's foundation. See also Sokolsky 1989; Moens 2012.
24 See the statements by Colonel Ian Hope in Day 2014.
25 Stein and Lang 2007, 192.
26 See McDonough 2009 for a less optimistic assessment of the impact on Canada's influence of its participation in this mission.
27 Fitzsimmons 2013.
28 Interview with Bill Graham, 19 April 2007, Ottawa.
29 See also Willis, "An Unexpected War" on this point.
30 Interview with Paul Martin.

31 To be clear, this view of many small Canadian contingents being displayed on UN maps may not be an accurate reflection of Canadian defence policy, but it was a view Martin espoused in my interview with him.

32 I served on the US Joint Staff's Directorate of Strategic Planning and Policy in 2001–2 and helped organize one of these meetings – called the Quint for the five countries making the major decisions: France, Germany, Italy, the United Kingdom, and the United States.

33 Nipa Banerjee, who wrote the CIDA evaluation comparing Herat and Kandahar, laments that she did not find the absence of development work in Kandahar to be a strong signal of future problems; interview with Nipa Banerjee, 17 May 2013, Ottawa.

34 Auerswald and Saideman 2014.

35 Willis, "An Unexpected War." See also Fenton 2007.

36 For a similar argument, that the CF was not as dominant and that the decision was in the hands of the politicians, see Middlemiss and Stairs 2008.

37 This may be induced by the structure of the Canadian political system – that it is the job of opposition parties to oppose, as Paul Martin told me in my interview with him. My response is that it is the job of opposition parties to criticize, but mindless gainsaying is both irresponsible and poor politics.

Chapter Four

1 Canada's most recent period of minority government before the Martin government of 2004 was 1979–80. The only overlap with war was the minority government that began in the summer of 1945, after Germany had been defeated but before Japan fell. See Lagassé 2010 for a discussion of what Parliament can and cannot do.

2 While holding such votes was consistent with the ideology of the Reform Party in the 1990s, Stephen Harper was hardly consistent in subjecting deployments to votes. He subjected combat missions to votes, but not non-combat deployments, with the result that the definition of *combat* became inconsistent. See Philippe Lagassé, "When Does Parliament Get to Vote on Military Deployments?" *Centre for International Policy Studies* (blog), 8 September 2014, http://cips.uottawa.ca/when-does-parliament-get-to-vote-on-military-deployments/h, accessed 3 May 2015.

3 This was expressed in the Conservative Party platform in the 2005–6 campaign. "Make Parliament responsible for exercising oversight over the conduct of Canadian foreign policy and the *commitment of Canadian*

Forces to foreign operations" (italics added); see Conservative Party of
Canada 2006, 45. For a short history of parliamentary votes and non-votes
when Canada deploys its forces, see this op-ed piece by John Ibbitson:
"Harper Should Allow a Vote on Deployment," *Globe and Mail*, 15 March
2006, http://www.theglobeandmail.com/news/world/harper-should-
allow-a-vote-on-deployment/article728406/, accessed 5 June 2013.

4 Despite the ideological commitment, Harper indicated that he would
extend the mission for a year even if the vote did not go his way – that
the vote would not limit his prerogative.

5 Nossal 2010. Bercuson and Granatstein (2011, 27) suggest that Harper
pushed for an approval vote rather than a "take note" debate to split the
Liberals.

6 John Manley asserted that the Liberals were already divided; interview,
22 August 2013, Ottawa.

7 Instead, the Netherlands had that experience in 2010, when its
Parliament failed to extend its mission in Uruzgan.

8 See Sjolander 2009.

9 Manley et al. 2008, 54.

10 Manley et al. 2008, 37.

11 Interview with John Manley.

12 Manley et al. 2008, 37–8.

13 Manley et al. 2008, 37.

14 Indeed, Manley and the other panel members intended to give each
party something to like so that they could support the overall report;
interview with John Manley.

15 Manley et al. 2008, 32 (italics added).

16 Nossal (2009) argues that the extension vote was not really about setting
a deadline, but I have the benefit of writing after 2011.

17 It was actually more complicated than that. France agreed to move its
contingent out of Kabul and into more violent Kapisa Province as the
new French President Sarkozy was more favourably disposed to helping
the United States than former president Chirac had been. The American
troops previously allotted to the Kapisa mission went to Kandahar
instead, meeting the Manley Panel's requirement.

18 More than 58 per cent of the CF members killed in Afghanistan were
victims of IEDs.

19 Philippe Lagassé first explained the notion of laundering accountability
in testimony to the House of Commons Standing Committee on National
Defence, 41st Parliament, 1st Session, Number 027, 16 February 2012,
http://www.parl.gc.ca/HousePublications/Publication.aspx?Language

=E&Mode=1&Parl=41&Ses=1&DocId=5395665&File=0#Int-6627509,
accessed 26 November 2013. See also Lagassé 2013.

20 Only in the 2011 election did the rise of the NDP and the collapse of the
Liberals signal the possibility that the Conservatives could win a
majority without any help from Quebec voters. To be clear, Quebec's
casualty aversion, like that of advanced democracies generally, is largely
overstated, but fears of such dynamics tend to cause politicians to
overreact. (See Chapter 8.)

21 For this story and others, see Martin 2010, especially Chapter 7 and
pages 117–8. For similar strategies on other issues, see Turner 2013.

22 Confidential conversation with senior official (Public Affairs branch,
DND), March 2008, Ottawa.

23 This policy was a product of the Somalia Affair in the mid-1990s.

24 The data for these figures are compiled from the Google News archives
and the Canadian Newsstand Complete database. News stories were
compared to make sure that events were counted only once.

25 At https://www.google.ca/trends/explore#q=afghanistan%20harper,
accessed 10 June 2013.

26 Canada, Parliament, House of Commons, *Debates*, 39th Parliament,
1st Session, Number 025, Government Orders – Canada's Commitment
in Afghanistan, 1710, Wednesday, 17 May 2006, http://www.parl.gc.ca/
HousePublications/Publication.aspx?Language=E&Mode=1&Parl=39&S
es=1&DocId=2215122-OOB-1543354, accessed 10 August 2015.

27 Canada, Parliament, House of Commons, *Debates*, 39th Parliament,
2nd Session, Number 064, Oral Questions – Afghanistan, 1415, Tuesday,
11 March 2008, http://www.parl.gc.ca/HousePublications/Publication.
aspx?Language=E&Mode=1&Parl=39&Ses=2&DocId=3349556-OOB-
2368881, accessed 10 August 2015.

28 Nossal 2009, 160.

29 New Democratic Party of Canada 2006, 44. It was only in 2011 that
the NDP supported a NATO effort – in Libya – as it was viewed as a
Responsibility to Protect mission, and even then, the party changed its
position after Jack Layton's death.

30 See Boucher and Roussel 2008, 141. See Chapter 8 for a discussion of
Quebec public opinion in contrast to the rest of Canada on the
deployments.

31 Canada, Parliament, House of Commons, *Debates*, 39th Parliament,
1st Session, Number 025, Government Orders – Canada's Commitment
in Afghanistan, 1640, Wednesday, 17 May 2006, http://www.parl.gc.ca/
HousePublications/Publication.aspx?Language=E&Mode=1&Parl=39&S
es=1&DocId=2215122-OOB-1543354, accessed 10 August 2015.

32 Canada, Parliament, House of Commons, *Debates*, 39th Parliament, 2nd Session, Number 063, Government Orders – Business of Supply, Opposition Motion – Afghanistan, 1315, Monday, 10 March 2008, http://www.parl.gc.ca/HousePublications/Publication.aspx?Language=E&Mode=1&Parl=39&Ses=2&DocId=3344423-OOB-2363367, accessed 10 August 2015.

33 For more on this effort to form a coalition, see Topp 2010.

34 *National Post*, "Stephen Harper's December 3, 2008 Statement," 3 December 2008, http://web.archive.org/web/20081207233751/http://www.nationalpost.com/news/politics/story.html?id=1028147, accessed 17 June 2013.

35 Nossal 2009.

36 See Bland and Rempel 2004 for a thorough argument about the historical weakness of Parliament when it comes to defence issues.

37 In areas of legislative authority, such as the budget or legislation, this may not always be the case.

38 Paul Martin, quoted from interview, 29 March 2007, Montreal.

39 In the language of social science, the collapse of the Liberals is "overdetermined." So much was going on that it is hard to separate the costs of their stance on the Afghanistan file from other dynamics occurring at the time, including the selection of leaders who were hardly adept (Dion, Ignatieff).

Chapter Five

1 Interview with Hon. Claude Bachand, 27 March 2007, Ottawa.

2 Interview with Paul Martin, 29 March 2007, Montreal.

3 Interviews with Senator Tommy Banks (member of the Special Committee on National Security and Defence), 4 November 2010, Ottawa; and Senator Colin Kenney, 7 June 2011, Ottawa. The problem of accountability in matters of national defence are more complicated than I can portray here. See Lagassé 2010 for a thorough discussion of these issues. For a more critical view, see Rempel 2002; Bland and Rempel 2004.

4 Bercuson 1996; Commission of Inquiry into the Deployment of Canadian Forces to Somalia 1997; Desbarats 1997.

5 Canada, Parliament, House of Commons, *Debates*, 39th Parliament, 1st Session, Number 003, Wednesday, 5 April 2006, to 41st Parliament, 1st Session, Number 068, Thursday, 15 December 2011, Oral Questions, http://www.parl.gc.ca/housechamberbusiness/ChamberSittings.aspx?View=H&Language=E&Mode=1&Parl=41&Ses=1, accessed October–November 2013. See also Figure 5.1.

6 Brewster 2011, 64–5. It also made it politically difficult in many countries to participate in OEF. Some parliaments enacted restrictions – caveats – limiting their contingents from cooperating with OEF while still participating in ISAF (Auerswald and Saideman 2014).

7 Interview with a senior adviser in Denmark's prime minister's office, August 2010, Copenhagen.

8 Centre for Military Studies roundtable, University of Copenhagen, 26 August 2010, which included Lars Bangert Struwe, Kristian Søby Kristensen, Henrik Breitenbauch, Esben Salling Larsen, and Mikkel Vedby Rasmussen.

9 Interview with Colonel Jan Swillens (former battle group commander), 27 January 2011, The Hague.

10 Interview with a German officer who had served on exchange with the Dutch, 15 June 2009, Berlin.

11 Interviews with Romanian representative at United States Central Command, 23–4 February 2009, Tampa.

12 Open Australia, House Debates, Thursday, 24 November 2011, "Ministerial Statements: Afghanistan," http://www.openaustralia.org/debate/?id=2011-11-24.5.2, accessed 27 March 2013.

13 *Sydney Morning Herald*, "Military Personnel Face Charges over Afghan Detainees: Smith," 10 May 2012, http://www.smh.com.au/opinion/political-news/military-personnel-face-charges-over-afghan-detainees-smith-20120510-1yeel.html, accessed 27 March 2013.

14 *BBC News*, "'Partial Victory' in Challenge to UK Taliban Transfers," 25 June 2010, http://www.bbc.co.uk/news/10412708, accessed 27 March 2013.

15 *BBC News*, "Detainees 'Risk Ill Treatment in Afghan Custody,'" 29 November 2012, http://www.bbc.co.uk/news/uk-20542831, accessed 27 March 2013.

16 For this document and others related to the detainee controversy, see "The Afghan Detainee Document Dump," Stephen Taylor (website), http://www.stephentaylor.ca/2009/12/the-afghan-detainee-document-dump/, accessed 15 July 2013.

17 Glyn Berry was the civilian head of the Canadian governance and reconstruction effort, and his death was a severe shock to Canadians both in Kandahar and back home.

18 Graeme Smith, "From Canadian Custody into Cruel Hands," *Globe and Mail*, 23 April 2007, http://www.theglobeandmail.com/news/world/from-canadian-custody-into-cruel-hands/article585956/?page=all, accessed 12 November 2013. Smith dedicates Chapter 8 of his book to his research on detainees being abused (Smith 2013).

19 See David Mulroney's explanation in his testimony to Parliament: Canada, Parliament, House of Commons, 40th Parliament, 2nd Session, Number 017, Special Committee on the Canadian Mission in Afghanistan, 1545, Thursday, 26 November 2009, http://www.parl. gc.ca/HousePublications/Publication.aspx?DocId=4266062&Language= E&Mode=1&Parl=40&Ses=2#Int-2978716, accessed 15 October 2013.

20 Kerry Wall, "Memorandum of Understanding on the Afghan Detainee Documents," *CBC.ca*, 16 June 2010, http://www.cbc.ca/newsblogs/ politics/inside-politics-blog/2010/06/memorandum-of-understanding-on-the-afghan-detainee-documents.html, accessed 15 October 2013. The NDP did not participate because it found this process to be insufficient.

21 Laura Payton, "Afghan Detainee Records Still Hold Questions, MPs Say," *CBC.ca*, 22 June 2011, http://www.cbc.ca/news/politics/story/2011/ 06/22/afghan-detainee-documents.html, accessed 15 October 2013.

22 This is admittedly speculation, but it seems logical that an empowered committee would have been able to request the documents and read them far faster than this process, which required a variety of actors to have their say before and after the subset of the committee could see the documents.

23 Interview with Tommy Banks, 26 November 2009, Ottawa. See also Bland and Rempel 2004, 25.

24 Canada, Parliament, House of Commons, *Debates*, 39th Parliament, 1st Session, Number 003, Wednesday, 5 April 2006, to 41st Parliament, 1st Session, Number 068, Thursday, 15 December 2011, Oral Questions, http://www.parl.gc.ca/housechamberbusiness/ChamberSittings.aspx? View=H&Language=E&Mode=1&Parl=41&Ses=1, accessed October–November 2013.

25 Question Period is stage-managed by each party (Bland and Rempel 2004, 20), so the onus for asking the wrong questions is really on the opposition parties.

26 This observation is not new, as Bland and Rempel (2004) made similar claims.

27 For instance, German defence committee members meet with the defence minister every week for classified briefings.

28 The exception to this seems to be defence procurement – the NDP's expertise on this issue and, as a result, its pressure on the government have been impressive.

29 Interview with Colin Kenney.

30 Gloria Galloway, "Is Canada's Party Discipline the Strictest in the World? Experts Say Yes," *Globe and Mail*, 7 February 2013, http://www.theglobe-andmail.com/news/politics/is-canadas-party-discipline-the-strictest-in-the-world-experts-say-yes/article8313261/, accessed 15 October 2013.

31 For a thorough discussion of these issues, see Lagassé 2010.
32 There is a bill that proposes to create some kind of committee whose members would possess security clearances, but it does not have the best of chances. The overwhelming focus for improving Parliament's information problem is on the intelligence agencies and not DND.

Chapter Six

1 In my research for a book on NATO, I interviewed policymakers, military officers, and scholars in Europe, Australia, and New Zealand, and, largely unsolicited, many expressed very positive views of the Canadian WG effort. For a piece that considers the origins of Canadian WG, see Desrosiers and Lagassé 2009.
2 I had a wonderfully amusing interchange with a group of junior army officers at a conference at the University of New Brunswick in January 2013, as I pointed out that the infantry could actually be seen as enablers for a navy or air force effort. (I didn't even mention civilians.)
3 I was part of a small group of academics whom DND and NATO led through Kabul and Kandahar in December 2007, and junior officers used this word during a briefing.
4 Telephone interview with David Mulroney, 18 July 2013.
5 United States Department of the Army 2007, 67.
6 Interview with Scott Gilmore (deputy for South Asia, DFAIT, in 2003), 14 June 2013, Ottawa.
7 Cox 2007.
8 Interview with Wendy Gilmour, 15 August 2013, Ottawa. This was fairly common across NATO as many countries simply did not have policies in place that would provide benefits and insurance similar to those enjoyed by their armed forces. Most caught up along the way but had started out quite unprepared.
9 Interview with David Mulroney.
10 See Brown 2008 for an assessment mid-way through the effort.
11 See the very telling remarks made by the anonymous former CIDA head, quoted in Jonathan Kay, "A Canadian Foreign-Aid Insider Explains Our $1.5 Billion Afghan Sinkhole," *National Post*, 13 October 2012. Brown (2015) captures well the various motivations and justifications of Canadian aid policy.
12 Interview with Nipa Bannerjee (CIDA representative, Canadian embassy, Kabul, from August 2003 to September 2006), 17 May 2013, Ottawa. She now teaches at the University of Ottawa's School of International Development and Global Studies.

13 Afghanistan has consistently been among the top 10 most corrupt
    countries in the world, according to Transparency International, http://
    www.transparency.org/country#AFG, accessed 30 July 2013 – not to
    mention that the former president's brother, Ahmed Wali Karzai, the
    power broker in Kandahar, was suspected of being a, if not the, criminal
    kingpin of southern Afghanistan.
14 Repeated by multiple interviewees.
15 Interview with a senior civilian in DFAIT, Ottawa, May 2011.
16 Interviews with, among others, Nipa Banerjee and Paul Larose-Edwards
    (executive director, CANADEM), 7 June 2011, Ottawa. I do not report
    interviews with CIDA personnel since they refused to talk to me.
17 Interviews with Glen Linden (International Affairs Division, Department
    of Public Safety) and Robert Mundie (Strategic Policy branch,
    Department of Public Safety), 7 June 2011, Ottawa.
18 Interview with David Muirhead (project coordinator, International Peace
    Operations branch, RCMP), 26 July 2011, Ottawa.
19 Interviews with Glen Linden and Robert Mundie.
20 The summary here is influenced by the account of Marten (2010) as well
    as that of Bercuson and Granatstein (2011).
21 St-Louis 2009.
22 Bercuson and Granatstein 2011.
23 Interviews with CF and DFAIT officers.
24 For more on the SAT-A, see Marten 2010.
25 Interview with Wendy Gilmour.
26 Brewster 2011, 177.
27 This paragraph relies heavily on my telephone interview with David
    Mulroney, 18 July 2013, but is also drawn from Hillier 2010, 466.
28 CIDA briefing note, "DM-Level Meeting on Afghanistan," 24 January
    2006, released under the Access to Information Act.
29 For an assessment of the impact of the Manley Panel on the PRT effort,
    see Leprince 2013.
30 Interview with Scott Gilmore.
31 David Mulroney, quoted from interview.
32 Interview with David Mulroney.
33 Mentioned in my interviews with David Mulroney and Elissa Golberg,
    7 June 2011, Ottawa. Golberg served not only as the first RoCK but also
    previously on the Manley Panel.
34 The archived quarterly reports can be found at http://epe.lac-bac.gc.ca/
    100/205/301/afghanistan/www.afghanistan.gc.ca/canada-afghanistan/
    documents/qr-rt.aspxlangeng.htm, accessed 2 January 2015.
35 Interview with Scott Gilmore.

36 US assessments leaked by WikiLeaks indicated that the dam project was tainted from the outset by ties to the Karzai family; see David Pugliese, "Expensive Legacy Sits in Murky Waters, Still under Construction," *Ottawa Citizen*, 18 February 2014, A1, A4.

37 Interview with David Mulroney.

38 Ibid.

39 Interview with a senior DFAIT government representative, May 2011, Ottawa. Bossenmaier did not have Mulroney's political connections, including access to Harper, or his tenacity or reputation.

40 Recent reports indicate that progress on the dam has been exaggerated; see Pugliese, "Expensive Legacy," A1.

41 Government of Canada 2012, http://epe.lac-bac.gc.ca/100/205/301/afghanistan/www.afghanistan.gc.ca/canada-afghanistan/documents/r06_12/index.aspxlangeng.htm, accessed 29 August 2015.

42 Ibid., 13. Italics added.

43 Graeme Smith devotes a chapter of his book to the first prison break, providing a fascinating account (Smith 2013). He sees these breakouts in much the same way I do – as cautionary tales about the larger effort.

44 Tunnelling out of prisoner of war camps is not just a topic for movies and television shows but has a long history in wars of the past.

45 Several critical stories emerged after the Canadians left; see, e.g., Paul Watson, "Canada's Afghan Legacy: Shoddy School Buildings and Sagging Morale," *Thestar.com*, 15 July 2012, http://www.thestar.com/news/world/2012/07/15/canadas_afghan_legacy_shoddy_school_buildings_and_sagging_morale.html, accessed 3 January 2015.

46 This is very much the opposite of what John Manley had advocated; interview, 22 August 2013, Ottawa.

47 Interview with Andrew Scheidl, who served in CEFCOM during much of this period, 22 August 2013, Ottawa.

48 Marten (2010) comes to similar conclusions.

49 Leprince 2013.

50 I have had multiple meetings and roundtables at DFAIT/DFATD.

51 Interview with Elissa Golberg; according to her, this had not been done before.

52 See my tale of the civilian lessons-learned exercise in Chapter 9.

53 Desrosiers and Lagassé (2009) argue that not only were there obstacles but that the entire emphasis on WG provided agencies with opportunities to defend their turf and extend themselves at the expense of their rivals.

54 I witnessed this first-hand during 2001–2. I had a Council on Foreign Relations International Affairs Fellowship, which placed me on the US

Joint Staff's Directorate of Strategic Planning and Policy – the key nexus between the US military and everybody else: government departments, NATO missions, defence attachés from around the world, and so on.

55 Interview with Ben Rowswell (former RoCK), 11 May 2011, Ottawa.

56 Including David Mulroney and Ben Rowswell. See also Marten 2010.

Chapter Seven

1 While senior officers' operational experience is often seen as a plus when they are being considered for promotion, many of Canada's allies do not have a similar record. For example, the selection of General Joseph Dunford to be the Chairman of the Joint Chiefs of Staff marks the first time that an Afghanistan/Iraq veteran was given the top spot in the United States, while General Jonathan Vance is the third CDS with recent operational experience in these places after generals Rick Hillier and Walt Natynczyk.

2 For an example of this contrast between Canadian generals and others, see David Pugliese, "Top Canadian General Defends Success of Afghan Campaign," *Ottawa Citizen*, 5 September 2013. This is, of course, still up for much debate, as depicted by Maloney 2013b. See also Paris 2014.

3 For more extensive discussions of the Canadian adaptation to Afghanistan, see Saideman 2013; Auerswald and Saideman 2014.

4 This refers to the beating death of a Somali teenager by the CF while it was engaged in peacekeeping in 1993; it led to a significant crisis within the CF and in civil-military relations (Bercuson 1996; Dawson 2007; Desbarats 1997).

5 Hillier 2010, 158–9.

6 Interview with Colonel (ret.) Pat Stogran (vice-president, Pearson Peacekeeping Centre), 25 April 2007, Ottawa.

7 Operation Anaconda was one of the few major operations in 2002 (Maloney 2005; Naylor 2005).

8 Interview with Major General Peter Devlin, 15 May 2009, Ottawa. He later became chief of the land staff. Calls home for permission sometimes took longer if the deputy chief of the defence staff (DCDS) had to consult with the CDS and perhaps the defence minister. The defence minister at the time, Bill Graham, did not recall having to give permission for any operations during Lt.-General Andrew Leslie's time; interview with Bill Graham, 19 April 2007, Ottawa.

9 DCDS Intent Task Force Kabul, 19 December 2003, A0241084, 6, acquired through an Access to Information request; italics added.

10 Interview with Brigadier-General Jocelyn Lacroix, 6 February 2007, Kingston.
11 Interview with General Rick Hillier (CDS), 11 March 2008, Ottawa.
12 Interview with Colonel Steve Noonan, 11 January 2007, Ottawa.
13 CDS Operational Order 800 (010/2005) Task Force Afghanistan, 11, acquired through an Access to Information request.
14 Horn 2010.
15 Interview with Brigadier-General David Fraser, 29 January 2007, Edmonton.
16 Commander's Directive to Commander, Task Force Afghanistan, Rotation 2 (3350-165/A37) A0232107, 14, acquired through an Access to Information request; italics added.
17 Among the officers commanding the Canadian task force in Kandahar, there is only one with whom I did not have an interview or series of conversations – Brigadier-General Daniel Menard, who was sent home prematurely due to his affair with a subordinate. For the sake of brevity, I do not include quotes from the series of Kandahar commanders.
18 Hillier 2010.
19 Several of the commands that Hillier set up were subsequently combined into Canadian Joint Operations Command (CJOC). CJOC, and thus the operational command of the CF efforts in the world, remains in suburban Ottawa, away from National Defence Headquarters. The most experienced Afghan hand, Lt.-General Jon Vance, replaced Lt.-General Stuart Beare as commander of CJOC in 2014.
20 Interview with Bill Graham, 19 April 2007, Ottawa.
21 Interview with Rick Hillier.
22 Interview with Vice-Admiral (ret.) Gregg Maddison, 19 June 2007, Montreal.
23 Said at an event held under the Chatham House Rule, Ottawa, 2008.
24 Operation Medusa was the first big NATO offensive aimed at disrupting the Taliban as the latter tried to encroach on Kandahar in the summer of 2006 (Horn 2010).
25 This was confirmed in multiple conversations, including one with a former adviser to Minister of National Defence Peter MacKay, spring 2014, Ottawa.
26 While Canadian leadership of American units has occurred elsewhere (in the North American Aerospace Defense Command, in the skies over Kosovo, in the seas in various NATO missions), it is particularly meaningful in ground combat.
27 To be clear, the CF gained influence at the operational level – by how it was deployed in Afghanistan – and not so much at the strategic level,

which included the larger purposes and outcomes that ISAF was seeking to achieve.

28 Hillier 2010.

29 The Canadians faced a burst of combat in the Balkans in the Medak pocket, but that did not resonate very much back home because of the largely successful efforts by the Chrétien government to keep that event secret (Off 2004).

30 Indeed, DND's "1994 White Paper on Defence" made it clear that combat was the CF's priority, https://www.civcap.info/fileadmin/user_upload/Canada/White_Paper_on_Defence_01.pdf, accessed 25 February 2014. Thanks to Philippe Lagassé for pointing this out.

31 Hillier 2010, 493–4.

32 Some examples are Major General Steve Bowes at the Conference on International Security, Kingston, June 2013; and Lt.-General Pete Devlin at the Gregg Centre–Combat Training Centre Annual Conference, Fredericton, January 2013.

33 Stein and Lang 2007.

34 An event held under Chatham House Rule, Ottawa, 2008.

35 In 1968, the Viet Cong launched a major offensive during the Tet holiday, penetrating many major South Vietnamese cities. While the offensive was countered successfully on the ground, it proved to be a political disaster for South Vietnam and the United States, ultimately ending President Lyndon Johnson's re-election campaign and swinging American public opinion to be more clearly against the war.

36 See Leprince 2015 for a discussion of this effort.

37 For more on the varied efforts by NATO members and partners, see Auerswald and Saideman 2014.

38 See Lagassé and Sokolsky 2009.

39 See, for instance, "PMO Scripted Afghan Mission Message: Records," *Canadian Press*, 7 June 2010, http://www.cbc.ca/news/politics/pmo-scripted-afghan-mission-message-records-1.915363, accessed 3 January 2015.

40 I had multiple conversations in 2015 with members of the media, who expressed frustration about how limited access had been to both the SOF soldiers on the ground and the pilots on their bases in Kuwait.

41 Operation Impact Technical Briefing, 26 January 2015, http://www.forces.gc.ca/en/news/article.page?doc=operation-impact-technical-briefing-26-january-2015/i55as1un, accessed 4 May 2015.

42 Matthew Fisher, "'Openness' over Combat with ISIS Bites Harper Government," *National Post*, 28 January 2015, http://news.nationalpost

.com/full-comment/matthew-fisher-openness-over-combat-with-isis-bites-harper-government, accessed 4 May 2015.

43 David Perry has written extensively on cuts to operational readiness; see, e.g., Perry 2014.

44 See Chapter 1, note 3.

45 Lee Berthiaume, "Canada's Libya Mission Cost Seven Times What MacKay Said It Did," *National Post*, 11 May 2012, http://news .nationalpost.com/2012/05/11/libya-mission-cost-seven-times-what-the-government-said-it-would-documents/, accessed 25 February 2014.

46 Murray Brewster, "Cost of Canada's Mission in Iraq, Syria Will Hit $528 Million in Coming Year," *Thestar.com*, 1 April 2015, http://www.thestar .com/news/canada/2015/04/01/cost-of-canadas-mission-in-iraq-syria-will-hit-528-million-in-coming-year.html, accessed 4 May 2015.

47 Perry 2014. This strategy was largely aimed at investing in securing the Canadian Arctic by supplying a new port, icebreakers, and other ships, but none of the commitments have been realized or are even close to fruition.

48 Stein and Lang 2007.

49 For the best expression of this, along with the prescience to suggest that Hillier's overreaching might ultimately lead to a backlash and reduced influence, see Lagassé and Sokolsky 2009.

50 John Manley reminded me that the Independent Panel on Canada's Future Role in Afghanistan did not have a military member, although it did have an officer as a consultant; interview, 22 August 2013, Ottawa.

51 While I have not talked to Stephen Harper about this decision, my conversations with those in DND, DFAIT, and elsewhere indicate that he did not consult the CF before making this decision. It was a surprise to many in this community as well as to NATO officials.

52 *Globe and Mail*, "Gen. Hillier Explains the Afghan Mission," 16 July 2005, http://www.theglobeandmail.com/commentary/gen-hillier-explains-the-afghan-mission/article1331108/, accessed 24 August 2013.

53 Hillier 2010.

54 Telephone interview with David Mulroney, 18 July 2013.

55 DND estimates that 635 were wounded in action and another 1,436 were injured in non-combat situations, http://www.forces.gc.ca/en/news/article.page?doc=canadian-forces-casualty-statistics-afghanistan/hie8w9c9, accessed 3 January 2015.

56 Interview with Ben Rowswell, 17 May 2011, Waterloo, Ontario. He clarified that other agencies had also gone beyond the six and the three because there was so very much to do.

57 Again, the deployment of CF-18s and the SOF minimizes these risks, compared to the deployment of a battle group in the midst of a insurgency.

58 Other events also caused divisions between the CF and Conservative politicians, especially the series of procurement challenges.

59 Lagassé (2009) argues that Hillier also undermined the gains of the military by being too outspoken.

Chapter Eight

1 The data come from surveys taken by Angus Reid over the course of the mission; see http://www.angusreidglobal.com/issue/afghanistan/, accessed 18 December 2013.

2 I have wondered whether the drop was due more to what the Canadians were doing – engaging in combat and killing – than taking casualties. Thus far, no study of public opinion has really been able to differentiate between these two aspects of combat. Boucher and Nossal (2015) suggest that the mission mattered given that support was higher before and after Kandahar.

3 I track only those killed in action rather than include those wounded as we do not have as clear and consistent information on the wounded, nor are these numbers widely reported. The yearly figures of those killed in action come from the iCasualties.org website.

4 I use "casualties" here instead of "killed in action" as it is less awkward, but the reality is that the public knew of and reacted to deaths in the field rather than injuries.

5 Veilleux-Lepage 2013.

6 Loewen and Rubenson 2010.

7 Boucher 2010. To be clear, Quebec's support for the war did increase when the regiment based in Quebec, the Van Doos, was deployed and suffered some casualties; see Ipsos, "As Quebec Regiment Suffers Losses in Afghanistan, Support in Quebec Receives a Boost," 25 August 2007, http://www.ipsos-na.com/news-polls/pressrelease.aspx?id=3615, accessed 30 January 2014. For more on Quebec, see Boucher and Roussel 2008; for very good graphs on the regional differences in public opinion, see Boucher and Nossal 2015.

8 Scholarship tends to show that casualties cause public support to drop when the various political parties are divided; see Larson 1996.

9 See Fletcher, Bastedo, and Hove 2009.

10 Nanos Report 2009.

11 Ibid. A poll taken the following year by another firm indicates that more
    Canadians believed that torture happened and that the Canadians (the
    CF, the prime minister, DFAIT, etc.) knew about it; see Ipsos, "Six in Ten
    (61%) Believe Detainees Handed Over to Afghans by Canadians Have
    Been Tortured," 10 May 2010, http://ipsos-na.com/news-polls/
    pressrelease.aspx?id=4777, accessed 5 November 2013.
12 In the Nanos survey, Alberta is combined with Saskatchewan and
    Manitoba into "Prairies," probably to keep the number of observations
    comparable; see ibid.
13 Ekos Politics, "Attention to Afghan Detainee Issue Fading but Scepticism
    of Government Remains," 25 March 2010, http://www.ekospolitics
    .com/index.php/2010/03/attention-to-afghan-detainee-issue-fading-
    but-scepticism-of-government-remains-march-25-2010/, accessed
    5 November 2013.
14 This fits with the larger picture that Boucher and Nossal (2015) depict of
    a public that was not that passionate one way or the other.
15 For a story that addresses the politics and dangers of embedding, see
    Levon Sevunts, "Reporters on Ground in Afghanistan Help Canadians
    Make Informed Choices," *Montreal Gazette*, 31 December 2009, http://
    www.montrealgazette.com/news/Reporters+ground+Afghanistan+help
    +Canadians+make+informed+choices/2397748/story.html, accessed
    12 November 2013.
16 See Blatchford 2009; Brewster 2011; Smith 2013.
17 Ipsos, "Canadians Assess the Canadian Media and Its Coverage of the
    Afghanistan Mission," 6 December 2006, http://www.ipsos-na.com/
    news-polls/pressrelease.aspx?id=3303, accessed 30 January 2014.
18 Decillia 2009.
19 Graeme Smith, "From Canadian Custody into Cruel Hands," *Globe and
    Mail*, 23 April 2007, http://www.theglobeandmail.com/news/world/
    from-canadian-custody-into-cruel-hands/article585956/?page=all,
    accessed 12 November 2013. See also Smith 2013.
20 Interview with Brett Boudreau, 6 June 2013, Ottawa. He had served as
    public relations adviser to the chairman of the NATO Military
    Committee (when the chairman was Canadian General Ray Henault)
    and director of communications in the Privy Council Office (Afghanistan
    Task Force).
21 Angus Reid Public Opinion 2010, 9.
22 Stein and Lang 2007, 289–90.
23 Boucher 2009, 2010.
24 Stephen Harper, quoted in Nossal 2008, 80.

25 Nossal (2008) argues that Australia and Canada have different cultures, which shape how their leaders respond to the deaths of those serving in their armed forces and help to account for Harper and his defence ministers not attending the ceremonies. But it does not account for the unpopular policy stances taken and then reversed.

26 Boucher 2009, 718.

27 The original URL was http://www.afghanistan.gc.ca/. However, most of the content of the website has been archived, making it hard (but not impossible) to find the documents that the Canadian government produced to sell the mission to the public. Here is a good starting point: http://epe.lac-bac.gc.ca/100/205/301/afghanistan/www.afghanistan. gc.ca/canada-afghanistan/documents/qr-rt.aspxlangeng.htm. Of course, the decision to archive the key documents is another example of poor messaging as it makes it harder for the public to look back at the war.

28 Indeed, when I toured Kabul and Kandahar in December 2007 with a group of academics on a trip organized by DND and NATO, we were told not to interact with the media. Of course, when we bumped into some reporters at the KAF, we engaged them in a long conversation in the media tent. The lesson, as always, is that academics are lousy at following orders.

29 This was reported to me in multiple interviews with individuals working in DFAIT, DND, and other departments.

30 DND organized tours of the NATO and Canadian missions in Afghanistan, referring to the participants as "opinion leaders." These tours frequently included academics; I went on one of these in December 2007 with a handful of other scholars.

Chapter Nine

1 See *Spiegel* Online, "Kunduz Bombing: German Court Drops Case over Civilian Deaths," 11 December 2013, http://www.spiegel.de/ international/germany/court-says-germany-not-responsible-for- damages-in-afghanistan-attack-a-938490.html, accessed 28 February 2014.

2 Rajiv Chandrasekaran, "A Brand-New U.S. Military Headquarters in Afghanistan. And Nobody to Use It," *Washington Post*, 10 July 2013, http://www.washingtonpost.com/world/national-security/a-brand- new-us-military-headquarters-in-afghanistan-and-nobody-to-use-it/2013/ 07/09/2bb73728-e8cd-11e2-a301-ea5a8116d211_story.html?wprss=rss_ homepage, accessed 28 February 2014. To be clear, stories are now coming out that the Canadian-built schools have significant problems;

see Paul Watson, "Canada's Afghan Legacy: Shoddy School Buildings and Sagging Morale," *Thestar.com*, 15 July 2012, http://www.thestar.com/news/world/2012/07/15/canadas_afghan_legacy_shoddy_school_buildings_and_sagging_morale.html, accessed 4 January 2015.

3　Again, 158 CF, a civilian PRT director, and a journalist as well as five Canadians engaged in the delivery of aid.

4　Again, to be clear, the CF has been engaged in such exercises, and their lessons will be disseminated. On the other hand, a visit to the web page of the army's Lessons Learned Centre (http://www.army-armee.forces.gc.ca/en/lessons-learned-centre/lessons-learned-index.page) indicates that the lessons are not available online but must be requested.

5　In previous requests, which were to DND, I always obtained the documents I was looking for, even if they were partially redacted. This time, when the relevant government agency was the Privy Council Office, I was utterly stonewalled – no document at all. The excuses that were used can be appealed, but that will take far longer that I would like. Indeed, it has been more than two years since I filed my appeal, and I have yet to see any results.

6　For a thorough discussion of discerning lessons, see Bercuson and Granatstein 2011. As a result of my frustration with the government, I shaped the theme of *Canada among Nations, 2015: Canada Intervening in Nations* to focus on lessons learned from past interventions; see Hampson and Saideman 2015.

7　Of course, the Liberals had been in power for so long that they may have forgotten how to be in Opposition.

8　Lagassé 2013.

9　Auerswald and Saideman 2014.

10　Interview with Colin Kenney, 7 June 2011, Ottawa.

11　In the United States, for example, the prospect of being "wire-brushed" by a congressional committee behind closed doors has been something that military officers seek to avoid, as I witnessed during my fellowship on the US Joint Chiefs of Staff in 2001–2. Of course, Congress has powers (line item spending, approval of officers) that make it something to fear, so just having closed hearings with informed parliamentarians may not matter as much in Canada. Understanding oversight is something I am now seeking to study further.

12　Lagassé 2010.

13　Appointments of this kind, in which an individual leads a task force but does not really have a department, are much more dependent on the support of superiors.

14 Interview with David Fraser, 29 January 2007, Edmonton.

15 I have had numerous conversations in the past couple of years with all kinds of Canadians – military and civilian – and the contrast remains stark. I cannot name individual DFATD officials as it would be bad for their careers.

16 See, e.g., http://www.journal.forces.gc.ca/vol14/no1/page19-eng.asp and http://www.theglobeandmail.com/globe-debate/was-our-afghan-saga-useless-or-worse/article16273850/.

17 Ipsos, "Marking 10th Anniversary of 9/11, Majority (57%) of Canadians Agree Terrorist Attacks Are Defining Socio-political Event of Their Lifetime," 11 September 2011, http://ipsos-na.com/news-polls/pressrelease.aspx?id=5316, accessed 16 January 2014.

18 Roland Paris (2014) and I agree on much, but he focuses more on the situation in Afghanistan.

19 The World Bank conducted a report on the National Solidarity Programme, the largest and perhaps most important non-military effort, and found mixed results; see Beath, Christia, and Enikolopov 2013. Others argue that many indicators, such as infant mortality, have greatly improved since before the intervention; see Lauryn Oates, "The War in Afghanistan Made the Country Better," *Huntington Post Canada*, 16 January 2014, http://www.huffingtonpost.ca/lauryn-oates/afghanistan_b_4608807.html.

20 I participated in an event on 15 January 2014 to promote my previous book (see Auerswald and Saideman 2014), and Lt.-General (ret.) Andrew Leslie articulated the notion that Canadian defence and foreign policy must be based on Canadian values and interests. This helped me frame this discussion.

21 This book was in the last stages of production when the refugee crisis exploded in Europe and in the media around the world in August and September 2015.

References

Angus Reid Public Opinion. 2010. "Just Over a Third of Canadians Support the Mission in Afghanistan." 22 October. Vancouver: Angus Reid Institute. http://angusreid.org/just-over-a-third-of-canadians-support-the-mission-in-afghanistan/.

Auerswald, David P., and Stephen M. Saideman. 2014. *NATO in Afghanistan: Fighting Together, Fighting Alone.* Princeton, NJ: Princeton University Press. http://dx.doi.org/10.1515/9781400848676.

Baum, Matthew A. 2002. "The Constituent Foundations of the Rally-Round-the-Flag Phenomenon." *International Studies Quarterly* 46 (2): 263–98. http://dx.doi.org/10.1111/1468-2478.00232.

Beath, Andrew, Fotini Christia, and Ruben Enikolopov. 2013. *Randomized Impact Evaluation of Afghanistan's National Solidarity Programme: Executive Summary of the Final Report.* Washington, DC: World Bank. http://documents.worldbank.org/curated/en/2013/09/18304187/randomized-impact-evaluation-afghanistans-national-solidarity-program-executive-summary-final-report.

Bercuson, David J. 1996. *Significant Incident: Canada's Army, the Airborne, and the Murder in Somalia.* Toronto: McClelland & Stewart.

Bercuson, David J., and Jack L. Granatstein. With Nancy Pearson Mackie. 2011. "Lessons Learned? What Canada Should Learn from Afghanistan." Calgary: Canadian Defence and Foreign Affairs Institute.

Bland, Douglas L., and Roy Rempel. 2004. "A Vigilant Parliament: Building Competence for Effective Parliamentary Oversight of National Defence and the Canadian Armed Forces." *Policy Matters* 5 (1). Montreal: Institute for Research on Public Policy.

Blatchford, Christie. 2009. *Fifteen Days: Stories of Bravery, Friendship, Life and Death from inside the New Canadian Army.* Toronto: Doubleday Canada.

Boucher, Jean-Christophe. 2009. "Selling Afghanistan: A Discourse Analysis of Canada's Military Intervention, 2001–08." *International Journal* 64 (3): 717–33. http://dx.doi.org/10.1177/002070200906400308.
– 2010. "Evaluating the 'Trenton Effect': Canadian Public Opinion and Military Casualties in Afghanistan (2006–2010)." *American Review of Canadian Studies* 40 (2): 237–58. http://dx.doi.org/10.1080/02722011003734753.
Boucher, Jean-Christophe, and Kim Richard Nossal. 2015. "Lessons Learned? Public Opinion and the Afghanistan Mission." In *Canada among Nations, 2015: Canada Intervening in Nations*, edited by Fen Osler Hampson and Stephen M. Saideman. Waterloo, ON: Centre for International Governance Innovation.
Boucher, Jean-Christophe, and Stéphane Roussel. 2008. "From Afghanistan to 'Quebecistan': Quebec as the Pharmakon of Canadian Foreign and Defence Policy." In *Canada among Nations, 2007: What Room for Manoeuvre?*, edited by Jean Daudelin and Daniel Schwanen, 128–42. Kingston and Montreal: McGill-Queen's University Press.
Brewster, Murray, ed. 2011. *The Savage War: The Untold Battles of Afghanistan*. Mississauga, ON: Wiley.
Brown, Stephen. 2008. "CIDA under the Gun." In *Canada among Nations, 2007: What Room for Manoeuvre?*, edited by Jean Daudelin and Daniel Schwanen, 91–107. Kingston and Montreal: McGill-Queen's University Press.
– 2015. "Canada's Development Interventions: Unpacking Motivations and Effectiveness in Canadian Foreign Aid." In *Canada among Nations, 2015: Canada Intervening in Nations*, edited by Fen Osler Hampson and Stephen M. Saideman. Waterloo, ON: Centre for International Governance Innovation.
Commission of Inquiry into the Deployment of Canadian Forces to Somalia. 1997. *Dishonoured Legacy: The Lessons of the Somalia Affair*. Report of the Commission of Inquiry into the Deployment of Canadian Forces to Somalia. 5 vols. Ottawa: Minister of Public Works and Government Services Canada. http://publications.gc.ca/site/eng/9.700365/publication.html.
Conrad, Lieutenant-Colonel John D. 2009. *What the Thunder Said: Reflections of a Canadian Officer in Kandahar*. Toronto: Dundurn Group / Canadian Defence Academy Press.
Conservative Party of Canada. 2006. "Stand Up for Canada." Federal election platform. Ottawa: Conservative Party of Canada. http://www.cbc.ca/canadavotes2006/leadersparties/pdf/conservative_platform20060113.pdf.

Corbett, Ron. 2012. *First Soldiers Down: Canada's Friendly Fire Deaths in Afghanistan*. Toronto: Dundurn Group / Canadian Defence Academy Press.

Cox, Jim. 2007. "Afghanistan: The Canadian Military Mission." Library of Parliament InfoSeries. Parliamentary Information and Research Service Publication PRB-07-19E. Ottawa: Parliamentary Information and Research Service.

Dawson, Grant. 2007. *"Here Is Hell": Canada's Engagement in Somalia*. Vancouver: University of British Columbia Press.

Day, Adam. 2014. "Why Things Are Seen: A Story of Blunders, Bombs, Broken Teeth and Bad Ideas." *Legion Magazine* (January/February).

Decillia, Brooks. 2009. "The Contested Framing of Canada's Military Mission in Afghanistan: The News Media, the Government, the Military and the Public." MSc diss., London School of Economics and Political Science.

Desbarats, Peter. 1997. *Somalia Cover-Up: A Commissioner's Journal*. Toronto: McClelland & Stewart.

Desrosiers, Marie-Eve, and Philippe Lagassé. 2009. "Canada and the Bureaucratic Politics of State Fragility." *Diplomacy & Statecraft* 20 (4): 659–78. http://dx.doi.org/10.1080/09592290903455774.

Fenton, Anthony. 2007. "PropAFghanda: The Battle for Canadian Hearts & Minds," *Briarpatch Magazine* (online), 31 May, http://briarpatchmagazine.com/articles/view/loves-labour-lost, accessed 12 August 2015.

Fitzsimmons, Dan. 2013. "Canada, the North Atlantic Treaty Organization (NATO), and the International Security Assistance Force (ISAF) in Afghanistan." *International Journal* 68 (2): 305–13. http://dx.doi.org/10.1177/0020702013494547.

Flavelle, Ryan. 2013. *The Patrol: Seven Days in the Life of a Canadian Soldier in Afghanistan*. Toronto: HarperCollins Canada.

Fletcher, Joseph F., Heather Bastedo, and Jennifer Hove. 2009. "Losing Heart: Declining Support and the Political Marketing of the Afghanistan Mission." *Canadian Journal of Political Science* 42 (04): 911–37. http://dx.doi.org/10.1017/S0008423909990667.

Friscolanti, Mike. 2006. *Friendly Fire: The Untold Story of the U.S. Bombing That Killed Four Canadian Soldiers in Afghanistan*. Mississauga, ON: Wiley.

Government of Canada. 2012. *Canada's Engagement in Afghanistan: Fourteenth and Final Report to Parliament*. Ottawa: Public Works and Government Services Canada. http://epe.lac-bac.gc.ca/100/205/301/afghanistan/www.afghanistan.gc.ca/canada-afghanistan/documents/r06_12/index.aspxlangeng.htm.

Haglund, David G. 1997. "The NATO of Its Dreams? Canada and The Co-operative Security Alliance." *International Journal* 52 (3): 464–82. http://dx.doi.org/10.2307/40203221.

Hampson, Fen Osler, and Stephen M. Saideman, eds. 2015. *Canada among Nations, 2015: Canada Intervening in Nations*. Waterloo, ON: Centre for International Governance Innovation.

Hillier, General Rick. 2010. *A Soldier First: Bullets, Bureaucrats and the Politics of War*. Toronto: HarperCollins.

Horn, Bernd. 2010. *No Lack of Courage: Operation Medusa, Afghanistan*. Toronto: Dundurn Press.

Jockel, Joseph T., and Joel J. Sokolsky. 2009. "Canada and NATO: Keeping Canada in, Expenses Down, Criticism Out ... and the Country Secure." *International Journal* 64 (2): 315–36. http://dx.doi.org/10.1177/002070200906400202.

Kreps, Sarah. 2010. "Elite Consensus as a Determinant of Alliance Cohesion: Why Public Opinion Hardly Matters for NATO-Led Operations in Afghanistan." *Foreign Policy Analysis* 6 (3): 191–215. http://dx.doi.org/10.1111/j.1743-8594.2010.00108.x.

Lagassé, Philippe. 2009. "A Mixed Legacy: General Rick Hillier and Canadian Defence, 2005–08." *International Journal* 64 (3): 605–23. http://dx.doi.org/10.1177/002070200906400302.

–   2010. "Accountability for National Defence: Ministerial Responsibility, Military Command and Parliamentary Oversight." *IRPP Study*, No. 4. Montreal: Institute for Research on Public Policy.

–   2013. "The Crown's Powers of Command-in-Chief: Interpreting Section 15 of Canada's Constitution Act, 1867." *Review of Constitutional Studies* 18 (2): 189–220.

Lagassé, Philippe, and Joel J. Sokolsky. 2009. "A Larger 'Footprint' in Ottawa: General Hillier and Canada's Shifting Civil-Military Relationship, 2005–2008." *Canadian Foreign Policy Journal* 15 (2): 16–40.

Larson, Eric V. 1996. *Casualties and Consensus: The Historical Role of Casualties in Domestic Support for U.S. Military Operations*. Santa Monica, CA: Rand Corporation.

Leprince, Caroline. 2013. "The Canadian-Led Kandahar Provincial Reconstruction Team: A Success Story?" *International Journal* 68 (2): 359–77. http://dx.doi.org/10.1177/0020702013494065.

–   2015. "Living among the Population in Southern Afghanistan: A Canadian Approach to Counterinsurgency." In *Canada among Nations, 2015: Canada Intervening in Nations*, edited by Fen Osler Hampson and Stephen M. Saideman. Waterloo, ON: Centre for International Governance Innovation.

Loewen, Peter John, and Daniel Rubenson. 2010. "Canadian War Deaths in Afghanistan: Costly Policies and Support for Incumbents." Working paper.

Maloney, Sean M. 2005. *Enduring the Freedom: A Rogue Historian in Afghanistan.* Lincoln: University of Nebraska Press / Potomac Books.

– 2009. *Confronting the Chaos: A Rogue Military Historian Returns to Afghanistan.* Annapolis, MD: Naval Institute Press.

– 2013a. *Fighting for Afghanistan: A Rogue Historian at War.* Annapolis, MD: Naval Institute Press.

– 2013b. "'Was It Worth It?' Canadian Intervention in Afghanistan and Perceptions of Success and Failure." *Canadian Military Journal* 14 (1): 19–31.

Manley, Hon. John, Derek H. Burney, Hon. Jake Epp, Hon. Paul Tellier, and Pamela Wallin. 2008. *Independent Panel on Canada's Future Role in Afghanistan.* Cat. no. FR5-20/1-2008. Ottawa: Public Works and Government Services Canada.

Marten, Kimberly. 2010. "From Kabul to Kandahar: The Canadian Forces and Change." *American Review of Canadian Studies* 40 (2): 214–36. http://dx.doi.org/10.1080/02722011003734720.

Martin, Lawrence. 2010. *Harperland: The Politics of Control.* Toronto: Viking Canada.

Martin, Paul. 2009. *Hell or High Water: My Life in and out of Politics.* Toronto: McClelland & Stewart.

Massie, Justin. 2009. "Making Sense of Canada's 'Irrational' International Security Policy: A Tale of Three Strategic Cultures." *International Journal* 64 (3): 625–45. http://dx.doi.org/10.1177/002070200906400303.

– 2013. "Canada's War for Prestige in Afghanistan: A Realist Paradox?" *International Journal* 68 (2): 274–88. http://dx.doi.org/10.1177/0020702013492500.

McDonough, David S. 2009. "Afghanistan and Renewing Canadian Leadership: Panacea or Hubris?" *International Journal* 64 (3): 647–65. http://dx.doi.org/10.1177/002070200906400304.

Middlemiss, Danford W., and Denis Stairs. 2008. "Is the Defence Establishment Driving Canada's Foreign Policy?" In *Canada among Nations, 2007: What Room for Manoeuvre?*, edited by Jean Daudelin and Daniel Schwanen, 66–90. Kingston and Montreal: McGill-Queen's University Press.

Moens, Alexander. 2012. "NATO and the EU: Canada's Security Interests in Europe and Beyond." In *Canada's National Security in the Post-9/11 World: Strategy, Interests, and Threats*, edited by David S. McDonough, 143–59. Toronto: University of Toronto Press.

Mueller, John E. 1973. *War, Presidents, and Public Opinion.* New York: Wiley.

Nanos Report. 2009. "Canadian Armed Forces Most Credible on Afghan Detainee Issue." 23 December. Ottawa: Nanos Research Group. http://www.nanosresearch.com/library/polls/POLNAT-W09-T407E.pdf.

Naylor, Sean. 2005. *Not a Good Day to Die: The Untold Story of Operation Anaconda*. New York: Penguin.

New Democratic Party of Canada. 2006. "Jack Layton: Getting Results for People." Federal election platform. Ottawa: New Democratic Party of Canada. http://www.cbc.ca/canadavotes2006/leadersparties/pdf/ndp_platform-en-final-web.pdf.

Nossal, Kim Richard. 2004. "Defending the 'Realm' – Canadian Strategic Culture Revisited." *International Journal* 59 (3): 503–20. http://dx.doi.org/10.2307/40203952.

– 2008. "The Unavoidable Shadow of Past Wars: Obsequies for Casualties of the Afghanistan Mission in Australia and Canada." *Australasian Canadian Studies* 26 (1): 91–124.

– 2009. "No Exit: Canada and the 'War without End' in Afghanistan." In *The Afghanistan Challenge: Hard Realities and Strategic Choices*, edited by Hans-Georg Ehrhart and Charles Pentland, 157–73. Queen's Policy Studies Series. Kingston and Montreal: McGill-Queen's University Press/Queen's Centre for International Relations.

– 2010. "Making Sense of Afghanistan: The Domestic Politics of International Stabilization Missions in Australia and Canada." Paper presented at a conference of the Association for Canadian Studies in Australia and New Zealand, University of New England, Armidale, NSW, 5 July.

Off, Carol. 2004. *The Ghosts of Medak Pocket: The Story of Canada's Secret War*. Toronto: Random House Canada / Vintage Canada.

Paris, Roland. 2014. "The Truth about Afghanistan." *Policy Options* online (March). http://policyoptions.irpp.org/issues/opening-eyes/paris/.

Patterson, Kevin, and Jane Warren, eds. 2008. *Outside the Wire: The War in Afghanistan in the Words of Its Participants*. Toronto: Random House Canada.

Perry, David. 2014. "The Growing Gap between Defence Ends and Means: The Disconnect between the Canada First Defence Strategy and the Current Defence Budget." Vimy Paper 19. Ottawa: Conference of Defence Associations Institute.

Rempel, Roy. 2002. *The Chatter Box: An Insider's Account of the Increasing Irrelevance of Parliament in the Making of Foreign Policy*. Toronto: Dundurn Press.

Saideman, Stephen M. 2013. "Canadian Forces in Afghanistan: Generational Change While under Fire." In *Military Adaptation in Afghanistan*, edited by Theo Farrell, Frans Osinga, and James A. Russell, 219–41. Stanford, CA: Stanford University Press.

Sjolander, Claire T. 2009. "A Funny Thing Happened on the Road to Kandahar: The Competing Faces of Canadian Internationalism." *Canadian Foreign Policy Journal* 15 (2): 78–98. http://dx.doi.org/10.1080/11926422.2009.9673488.

Smith, Graeme. 2013. *The Dogs Are Eating Them Now: Our War in Afghanistan*. Toronto: Knopf Canada.

Sokolsky, Joel J. 1989. "A Seat at the Table: Canada and Its Alliances." *Armed Forces & Society* 16 (1): 11–35. http://dx.doi.org/10.1177/0095327X8901600103.

Stein, Janice Gross, and Eugene Lang. 2007. *The Unexpected War: Canada in Kandahar*. Toronto: Viking Canada.

St-Louis, Lieutenant-Colonel Michel-Henri. 2009. "The Strategic Advisory Team in Afghanistan – Part of the Canadian Comprehensive Approach to Stability Operations." *Canadian Military Journal* 9 (3): 58–67.

Topp, Brian. 2010. *How We Almost Gave the Tories the Boot: The Inside Story Behind the Coalition*. Toronto: James Lorimer.

Turner, Chris. 2013. *The War on Science: Muzzled Scientists and Wilful Blindness in Stephen Harper's Canada*. Vancouver: Greystone Books.

United States. Department of the Army. 2007. *The U.S. Army/Marine Corps Counterinsurgency Field Manual*. U.S. Army Field Manual no. 3-24: Marine Corps Warfighting Publication no. 3-33.5. Chicago: University of Chicago Press.

Veilleux-Lepage, Yannick. 2013. "The Implications of the Sunk Cost Effect and Regional Proximity on Public Support for Canada's Mission in Kandahar." *International Journal* 68 (2): 346–58. http://dx.doi.org/10.1177/0020702013492536.

Wattie, Chris. 2008. *Contact Charlie: The Canadian Army, the Taliban and the Battle That Saved Afghanistan*. Toronto: Key Porter.

Windsor, Lee, and David A. Charters. 2008. *Kandahar Tour: The Turning Point in Canada's Afghan Mission*. Mississauga, ON: John Wiley & Sons.

Wiss, Captain Ray. 2010. *A Line in the Sand: Canadians at War in Kandahar*. Vancouver: Douglas & McIntyre.

Zyla, Benjamin. 2013. "Explaining Canada's Practices of Burden-Sharing in the International Security Assistance Force (ISAF) through Its Norm of 'External Responsibility.'" *International Journal* 68 (2): 289–304. http://dx.doi.org/10.1177/0020702013493756.

Index

Page references followed by *fig* indicate a figure or a table.